Updated
With Strength Coaching Tools

Published by Integrity+ Consulting

24 Dewitt Court, Markham, Ontario, Canada L3P 3Y3

Phone: (905) 294-0380

E-mail: info@integrity-plus.com

Library and Archives Canada Cataloguing in Publication

Habashy, Baha, 1942-

Christ Centered Coaching: Thoughts and Tools from an Imperfect Coach / Baha Habashy with Margaret Habashy.

ISBN 978-0-9939302-3-2

Also available in Spanish –
Cristo de Coaching Centrado: Los pensamientos y las herramientas de un imperfecto
ISBN 978-0-9939302-4-9

Note: For readability and ease when referring to client or coach we use "he and him" instead of "he/she and him/her."

Table of Contents

INTRODUCTION

Writing about the Christian life, the Apostle Paul uses the metaphor of running in a race. Athletes all around the world appreciate the value of personal coaching. The same applies to each of us in the game of life with its challenges and uncompromising demands.

As Christians our life is centered by our relationship with Jesus Christ and His Spirit within us. God the Father has given each of us strengths to equip us to win and fulfill our life purpose and callings. If we are to excel and be the best we can be, we cannot escape the need for the training and coaching in the critical aspects of our life.

Dr. Albert Winseman, pastor, author and Senior Executive Coach with the Gallup organization, says, *"Everyone needs a coach and every one can coach."* Coaching trainer and author, Tony Stoltzfus, offers a course titled Peer Coaching. He says that coaching is *"a relational structure where two or three friends meet regularly for a clear purpose to help each other grow."* The Bible tells us that *"as iron sharpens iron so one man sharpens another."* Proverbs 27:17. This is Christ Centered Coaching. Later we will highlight that coaching is at the heart of making disciples.

As we write this booklet, we are most grateful for the many people who invested in coaching us through many challenges and various stages of life. Without their investment these pages would not have been written.

This booklet is written to encourage and foster coaching relationships in the church and community. Our objective is that it would serve as a catalyst in three different settings to:

- be an encouragement to use your God-given strength as a coach

- serve as an introductory tool that coaches can give to ind viduals seeking their help

- help each of us prioritize our need for coaches as we navigate the challenges of life and fulfill our life callings

About Change

Life is all about change. We must change as we grow. We need to adjust as the world changes around us. How we respond to our changing world is critical to our wellbeing. Like a good parent God desires healthy change for His children. God delights in seeing His children grow as they respond to their changing world.

But change is often not easy. Stop and think. Think back of times when you heard a good message or read about a good change that you wanted to apply in your life. How often did you follow through and make such change? Don't worry. You are not alone. To change we often need help.

The Professional Life Coaching course offered by Light University reports that the probability of someone acting on a good idea after hearing it or reading it is less than **10%**. That percentage changes to:

- **25%** if the person **commits** to apply the desired change

- **40%** if the person commits **to when** he is going to make the needed change.

- **50%** if the person **develops a plan** to act towards the desired change

- **65%** if the person **shares his plan** with another person. This illustrates the value of small group ministries in the church.

- **95%** if the person has ongoing predefined appointments with one other person to review ongoing progress and follow up on the plan. This illustrates the value of one-on-one coaching.

When we face life challenges or want to take advantage of great opportunities, most of us need support, encouragement, and/or accountability to help us achieve the desired change. In Christ Centered Coaching the coach partners with God in helping others move from **idea** to **desired** change to **willingness** to change and then to the **ability** to change.

- **Idea to change:** Nothing happens without an idea, a vision or a dream that relates to a need or opportunity of doing something good.

- **Desire to change:** The desire to change happens when we either envision the benefits of change or the negative consequences of continuing our life without change.

- **Willingness to change:** Change has a price. Willingness to change happens when we are willing to pay the price of change. The price for change is directly related to the expected benefits or the cost avoidance associated with the change.

- **Ability to change:** Ability to change goes beyond willingness and price to change. This is often related to cultural factors or elements beyond personal controls.

To illustrate the difference between idea, desire, willingness and ability to change, let me tell you about Pastor Sam[1]. Pastor Sam first contacted me because he had an idea. He heard that I help people with the problem of e-mail overload. During our initial conversion Sam told me he spends so much time on e-mail and finds it a waste of time. Our conversation uncovered the real cause of his overloaded life. Under his leadership the church has experienced 400% growth. Now he works more than 75 hours a week and seldom takes a day off. Although the church added two more pastors, his pastoral role has not changed much.

During our conversation Sam could see that his problem was **"Overload roles"** much more than e-mail overload. Through our conversation Sam began to see that he needs to make changes to his roles and work life, but he was not totally convinced about that idea. Ending our meeting, we agreed to meet again in few weeks. I left him with two discovery questions.

1. If solving your overload problem saved you 10 hours a week, what would you do with that time?

2. What will happen if you do not change your present workload?

During our follow-up meeting Sam told me that other than working, he had a hard time envisioning what he would do with any spare time. For more than 20 years in the same church, his life was totally focused around his work. He loved his work and would not desire any change.

For the second question, he said, "Thinking of what would happen if I do not change frightened me." As we talked Sam told me his medical profile has put him at a very high risk of a heart attack. His doctor and

---

[1] True story modified for illustration.

his wife have warned him repeatedly. His younger brother died leaving behind three fatherless children. As he pondered this, Sam began to move from **idea** to change to **desire** to change and **willingness** to change.

As we talked about the needed change he said, "Change will be hard but I am willing to do it." We agreed that I would help Sam in a three month coaching project to reduce his work life to no more than 60 hours a week. This would require a change in his church roles and responsibilities.

In addition, we talked about ways to help him envision what he would do with the time saved. For that with the help of his wife, we reorganized his office and placed large framed pictures of fun times with his family. We also added one framed picture of his deceased brother with his family.

During our regular meetings Sam made significant progress not only in how he handled e-mail but more importantly, managing meeting overload, phone calls, and endless interruptions that robbed him of valuable time. While hard and uncomfortable, he developed the skill of saying **"no"** to unrealistic demands and expectations. Pastor Sam moved from desire to change to willingness to change.

Regretfully, Pastor Sam had to confront the "ability to change." Initially, the leaders and the church board seemed to be understanding and supportive of the needed change. Unfortunately, over time influential church members began to complain and Sam began to lose the support of key board members. The church culture proved to be a major obstacle to change. Although Sam was able to achieve a sincere willingness to change, **ability to change** was much harder to conquer.

.

About us

As you read the following thoughts please note that **we are imperfect coaches at best**. We are not educated in the field of psychology or counseling. We do not have any coaching designation or certification. Our thoughts are based on long-lived lives, books we have read, lessons our clients have taught us, and the models of people who have invested in our lives and been our coaches through diverse careers, parenting, and more than 40 years of married life.

You may wonder how we started in coaching. When we started our independent consulting practice in 1999 we expected our focus to be on the field of knowledge management and related organizational change. As a small consulting practice we focused on clients where we could be the most objective and where we could bring the greatest value. We were privileged to work with clients as large as IBM as well pastoral teams in large and small churches. We often focused on the individuals we worked with much more than the organizations that paid our fees.

Over time some of our clients began to refer to us as coaches and mentors. As our clients continued to compliment us on our coaching and facilitation skills, we were compelled to learn more about what this title means to our clients and how we could offer such services with trust and integrity.

With this in view we searched the web, read books, and sought the counsel of knowledgeable friends and clients who became our advisors. The results are the thoughts and tools you will find in the following pages. While this was a good fit for our style and the needs of our clients, it may not be a good fit for others.

The Bible says, *"As iron sharpens iron, so one man sharpens another."* We all have opportunities to help someone in need of support, encouragement, and accountability. **This is the heart of coaching**. As we share our limited thoughts, tools, and experience with you, our hope is that you may be encouraged to coach someone.

The thoughts and tools in the following pages are a simple introductory resource for those who seek to help and coach others.

It is important that you prayerfully discern when additional professional training is needed.

As a coach it is your responsibility to encourage those you help to seek appropriate professional coaching, counselling or therapy when needed.

What Does Coaching Look Like?

Every coaching experience is different because every coach brings his or her unique talents, strengths, and style and every client brings his unique strengths and needs. Here are two examples.

About Kam

I, Baha, met Kam[1] at a business function. He was the Vice President of Sales and Marketing at a computer company. We connected as we compared his computer business to the way it was when I started my computer career 30 years earlier. He told me that he never thought he would be in the computer business. While growing up, sports were all he lived for. His physical build and competitive spirit gave him an easy ticket to a very successful but short career as a professional Football player. Unfortunately, a major injury put an end to his competitive sports and all the wealth and fame it brought. *"I think they hired me to sell computers because of my name not because of my brains,"* he said.

Before we parted I had a sense that he wanted to talk some more.

> **Baha:** Would you like to get together some time?
>
> **Kam:** Yeah, how about breakfast. There is a nice place near my office where I often go…

With that we confirmed a date for two weeks later.

When I got to the breakfast place, Kam was already working on his computer. After the normal greeting and chat about the weather I asked.

> **Baha**: *How are you Kam?*
>
> **Kam:** *I'm fine.*
>
> **Baha:** *This does not sound convincing.*

His tone of voice and his facial expression told me otherwise.

> **Baha:** *Kam, let me do something I do with my friends.*

How Are You?

- ☐ Physically
- ☐ Financially
- ☐ Emotionally
- ☐ Spiritually

With that I reached into my wallet and pulled my "How are you gauge" (See card image).

> **Baha:** *This card is what I call my **'How are you gauge".** Here is the deal. There are four words on this card: Physically, Emotionally, Financially, and Spiritually. You have to give me an honest number on how you feel on a scale of 1-5. We do not have to talk about anything unless you choose to.*

CHRIST CENTERED COACHING

Kam looked at this simple card for about 30 seconds, then said,

> **Kam:** *"Financially, no problem, five, I have all the money I will ever need. Physically, I am very tired. I work 60 - 70 hours a week. I do not sleep much but I do not need much sleep. My wife and kids are into sports. Any spare time I have I am at some sports event or driving them places. You know how it is."*
>
> **Baha:** *Yeah, I understand. I have been there.*
>
> **Kam:** *Emotionally I would give it 1 or less. Spiritually, I do not relate to that at all.*

Over eggs toast and coffee we talked for over an hour. Not really. Kam talked while I listened. He talked about unrealistic work demands and the deteriorating relationship with his wife. Occasionally I interjected with simple leading questions that started with what, why, how, when…

> **Baha:** *Kam before we leave, would you like make some changes to help you improve how you feel emotionally?*
>
> **Kam:** *Yeah, for sure…*
>
> **Baha:** *Would you like us to commit to a short term coaching relationship with the purpose of helping you make the changes you need to make?*
>
> **Kam:** *Yeah, that would be great*
>
> **Baha:** *Let me send you some thinking exercises to help you think through stuff and then I will give you a call to see how we can go from there.*

Following this conversation I e-mailed Kam some thinking exercises. *(See Sample Coaching Tools and Exercises)* This was the start of a three month purpose driven coaching relationship. Every two weeks we met for our coaching conversation. Before every meeting Kam sent me his Progress Dashboard (*See sample Progress Dashboard*) which provided the agenda for our Client Directed coaching relationship.

Now, what did I do for Kam? This may be best answered through the thank you note he sent me. It read:

> *"…you have succeeded in really **understanding where my challenges lie**, and as such **have pushed me to be accountable to those necessary changes** that I wouldn't have been able to see on my own. … You helped me realize my potential both personally and professionally, something I was not able to do until now."*

The truth is that Kam was an easy client to work with. He had experienced the advantages, disciplines, support, and accountability coaching brought to his sporting career. By asking questions I helped Kam see that he had the strengths and ability to make the changes he desired. Having said this, the same process, while slightly modified, could be the experiences of many coaches in many parts of the world.

Why Is Coaching Needed?

In recent years "coaching" has become a very popular term. In North America Life Coaching and Executive Coaching may be the fastest growing segment in the professional services field. You may wonder why. From our experience we suggest that there are many reasons such as the restructuring of family life and the shift in employee/employer relationships. Let us explain.

In previous generations the extended family played vital coaching and mentoring roles. Younger people relied on older family members for insight, support, and accountability. With migration and the disintegration of extended family bonds access to this vital role diminished. At the same time, life increased in complexity placing heavier burdens on both young and old.

On the business side, there has been a dynamic shift in the level of commitment and loyalty. The mentoring relationships that existed in the apprentice model have diminished if not totally gone. Business leaders see themselves as managers assigned to make the best of the employees under their authority. On the other hand, employees see themselves as a human resource available to the highest bidder with very short term commitment to their existing employer and limited expectations of coaching and/or mentoring. Even when managers have a desire to play a mentoring role, time constraints and/or lack of training stand as major stumbling blocks.

Having said this it is obvious that in families there are exceptions that should be celebrated. In the workplace more and more organizations encourage and compensate managers who demonstrate a coaching relationship with their staff. Many organizations acknowledge the need for a range of coaching and counseling services and pay for such services when accessed by their staff. In the community the church has a vital opportunity to offer a vast range of counseling and coaching ministries.

Coaching is one of the many services offered under a much broader umbrella of helping services that includes consulting, facilitation, counseling, mentoring, pastoral and spiritual care including spiritual directors. Books are written, courses are taught and degrees are granted to help provide qualification to provide an ever more specialized field. The following provides some simple descriptions:

- **Coaching:** Starting from the present state of mind and wellbeing and building on the client's intrinsic strengths, coaching focuses on the future aspirations, hopes, and dreams of the client.

- **Counseling:** Focusing on emotional or relational health, counseling enters into the field therapy or treatment and employs psychological or diagnostic assessment and therapeutic tools. Counseling often starts by dealing with the consequences of emotional hurts or conflicts resulting from trauma, miscommunication, and physical or emotional abuse.

- **Consulting:** A consultant is expected to evaluate, assess options, and recommend change. He is often expected to bring an added level of expertise, knowledge or experience in a special field. The consultant is often expected to make proposals for change and may play a key part in making the change happen.

- **Facilitation:** Facilitation takes many forms. At its heart it resembles coaching. The difference is that it often deals with helping groups of people achieve a desired change.

- **Mentoring:** This is often a longer term personal developmental partnership in which a more experienced or more knowledgeable person becomes a role model helping to guide a less experienced or less knowledgeable person. Another term that may be used in such a relationship is "Apprenticeship."
https://en.wikipedia.org/wiki/Mentorship - cite_note-MasteryWorks-1

- **Spiritual Director:** Similar to coaching the Spiritual Director is inclined to have a special focus on the disciplines required for a vibrant relationship with God.

- **Pastoral Care**: This is most often reflected in a clergy relationship. While some pastors are inclined to play many of the roles listed above, recently it is becoming more advantageous for pastors to act as the wise point of entry to many of these services. In a way it is best when the pastor helps the client identify his needs and then refers him to other providers who are better skilled or equipped to offer the related services.

The above list is not all encompassing. With the increasing challenges and complexities of our world, you are likely to find new and or renewed definitions and classifications.

Because of the vast range of services offered in this field, the role of a Coach is often ambiguous and outcomes are seldom documented. This has brought about the increased risks of miscommunication, misunderstanding or setting unrealistic expectations.

You can coach. You do not need a title to be a Coach. If you care about people then you can Coach. If you lead people it is your duty to Coach them. Jack Welsh, the former chairman of General Electric, is considered one of the best leaders of the 20th century. He said, "*If you do not coach your people, you should never be promoted.*" This highlights the growing need for managers to take personal interest in coaching their staff.

About Coaching Styles

For the purpose of our discussion we would like to define coaching as a "trusting, purpose driven, highly personal relationship between a "**Coach**" and another person we will call a **"Client"**. Coaching unlocks the Client's hidden potential and uses the unique talents that already exist within them. A coaching relationship primarily benefits the Client, but can have secondary benefits for the Client's organization or community.

The following diagram provides an alternate definition of coaching. It may be helpful to examine coaching on a spectrum from **directive and non-directive** and ranging from **high to low levels of authority.**

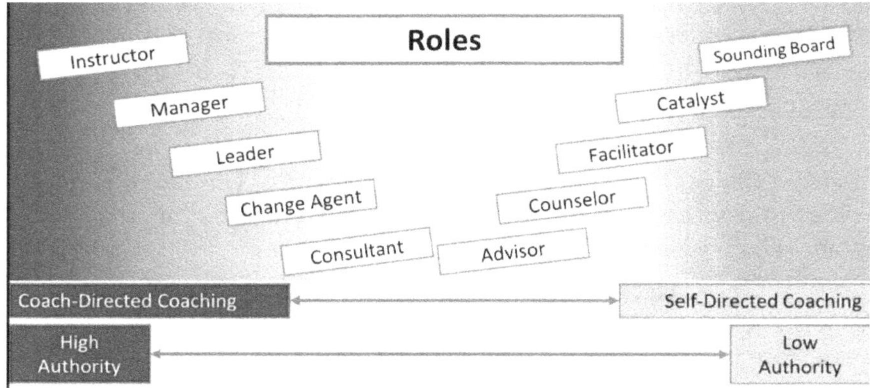

- **Directive Coaching:** This end of the scale is exemplified by the teacher or the authoritarian instructor. Here, the Coach relies heavily on his knowledge, competency, and experience to **direct the Client's activities** in fulfilling agreed-upon objectives. In this role, the Coach is invested with a high degree of **authority,** and demands adherence to specific instructions. Directive Coaching applies to those managers and leaders who seek to aggressively coach their staff. This is also useful, to a lesser degree, for consultants who are paid to deliver tangible results in the service of their Clients.

- **Non-directive Coaching:** On the other end of the scale, Non-Directive Coaching seeks to enable the Client to rely on his own knowledge, skills, and experience to fulfill agreed-upon objectives. Here, success does not rely on the Coach's knowledge or authority, but on his ability to facilitate the best outcome - based on the Client's own internal resources. Describing the role of such a Coach, author and coaching expert, Myles Downey, writes,

"The primary function of the Coach is to understand. Not to solve, heal, make better, or be wise... ...The magic is that it is in that moment of understanding that the player (Client) understands for himself, becomes more aware, and is then in a position to make better decisions and choices than he would have done anyway. This is how Coaching is profoundly simple and simply profound." [2]

Non-directed Coaching is not passive. With skillful questions that lead to understanding, the Coach brings out the Client's hidden creativity and insights. It is good to note that, to be most effective and gain needed trust, Client-Directed Coaching should be stripped of the perception of authority, while still having freedom to provide advice and accountability. This kind of coaching is the hallmark of successful managers and leaders who seek to empower and develop their teams.

This paper will focus on a non-directive coaching model that we call Client-Directed Coaching. This is a coaching relationship where the **client directs the objectives and goals and the coach controls the process and the needed tools**.

The attached diagram illustrates the foundations of Christ Centered Coaching relationships. Christ centered coaching is a three way partnership between a **COACH**, a **CLIENT** and **JESUS CHRIST**. Christ's Spirit empowers the **coach's** strengths and motivation to help the

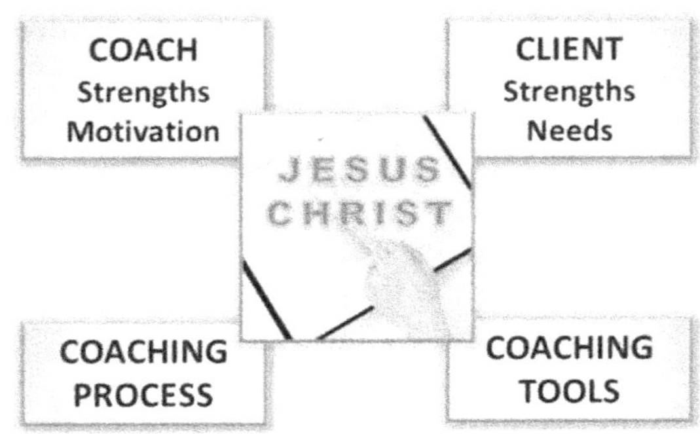

client discover his own strengths and respond to his own needs. This is an intentional, disciplined **PROCESS** supported by adequate thinking and communication **TOOLS**.

The practice of coaching is not limited to the Christian community. Both Christian and non-Christian coaching are purpose driven relationships where a **coach** uses his strengths to serve a **client,** using appropriate **tools** and **process.** However, from a Christian viewpoint we cannot overlook the role Jesus plays in this vital exchange.

Humanly speaking, it is impossible to aspire for a perfect coaching relationship. Why? Coaches and clients are imperfect people. Coaching tools and processes are man-made and imperfect at best. As illustrated in the attached diagram, there will always be a gap between these four parts that form a coaching relationship. This is the truth about all coaching relationships. The difference in Christ centered coaching is that the all-knowing, all wise Christ steps in and with wisdom bridges the gap. Jesus is intimately interested in and invested in every Christ centered coaching relationship.

Why? Jesus came that each of us may **"have life abundant."** The purpose of effective Christian coaching is to help the client enjoy this abundant life. This is an objective that cannot be achieved without the presence of Christ in the coaching relationship.

God has a clear purpose for each life. His purpose was revealed in creating us in His own image so we can do good work and have a personal relationship with Him. This was modeled for us in the life of Jesus

> Jesus said that if two or three are gathered in His name He would be there. He is the third participant in every coaching meeting.
>
> At the beginning of a coaching meeting we often ask the client to state the meeting goal in prayer asking Jesus for the specific results he would like to accomplish through a specific coaching session.

Christ. With His Spirit at the center of our life Christ gives us the freedom to make daily choices as we fulfill our life callings. The coach's job is simply to work with Christ to help the client discover, articulate, communicate, and fulfill God's purpose in these choices.

In Matthew 28:19-20 Jesus commanded His disciples to *"Go and make disciples of all nations … teaching them to obey everything I have commanded you. And surely **I am with you always**, even to the end of the age."*

Coaching is a critical part of making disciples. By His life and ministry Jesus provided a wonderful model that can be applied to today's coaching relationships. Jesus promised that He will never leave us. By His spirit He is present and ready to impact every coaching meeting.

Effective coaching seeks to discover the truth and the reality of the client's need. The coach's job is to help the client define an action plan that is built of truth and a way of fulfilling this plan. Jesus said, *"I am the truth and the way and the life…"* In a world that feeds lies and falsehood about who we are and what we should do, it is great to know that Jesus is part of every coaching conversation. He is able to reveal the truth and the way for change that can help the client find abundant life.

We suggest that the principles and foundations of effective coaching find their origins in the life, ministry, and model of Jesus Christ. Jesus desires that each of us become intentional in coaching and making disciples.

We are stewards of the lessons learned through our life journey with Jesus. Paul affirms this in his communication with Timothy as he says, *"…be strong in the grace that is in Christ Jesus. And the things you have heard me say in the presence of many witnesses entrust to reliable men who will also be qualified to teach others."* 2 Timothy 2:1-2.

Christ centered coaching fulfills God's desire for both coach and client. While the focus is the needs of the client, as a co-laborer with Christ, and by dependence on the spirit of Christ, the coach will grow to become more like Christ.

Know your strengths. The most important part in coaching is ensuring the right fit between coach and client. Effective coaching starts with understanding your strengths and knowing your spiritual gifts and how they relate to your role as a coach. Based on the parable of the talents in Matthew 25, effective Christian coaching is a stewardship of what you are given. An effective coach coaches out of his own talents and builds on the strengths God has given him.

I often wonder, along with fasting and praying, what Jesus did during His 40 days in the wilderness. This was an intense period of preparation for His new roles and ministry. We know that while He was all divine He was all human.

I wonder if He spent a great amount of time examining His roles in light of the gifts, talents, and the authority He was given. In His mind's eye He developed short and long term plans for how He will meet His disciples and what He will do during his limited time with them. He also knew that there will be lots of time when He will have to call on The Father for help and extra resources. I suspect He spent a lot of time reflecting on the Scriptures and the promises of God to support Him when he would be tired, disappointed, and even tempted. Yes, even Jesus Had to reflect on what motivated Him to carry on this arduous and challenging ministry.

About Strengths

As a coach you must know your strengths so you can clearly define the roles you are called to play in the lives of your clients. Based on the field of Strengths Psychology your strengths are the result of a formula illustrated in the attached diagram.

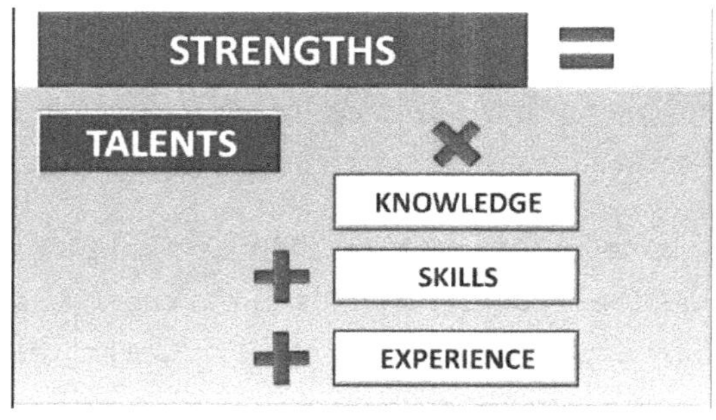

The scientists at the Gallup Organization define **strengths** as *"the ability to provide consistent, near-perfect performance in a given activity."* They also suggest that strengths start with **talents** that are defined as: *"naturally recurring patterns of thoughts, feelings or behaviors that can be productively applied."* Your talents are God's gift to you. God starts the process of giving you your talents long before you were born.

These talents are developed by the **knowledge** each of us acquires through the learning process in the school of life. In the school of life you also acquire the **skills** or the steps needed to apply the knowledge you have gained. **Experience** is the varied application of your talents, knowledge, and skills to diverse life circumstances. Through that process we develop what really matters, **wisdom. An effective coach is a wise coach**.

Just as your fingerprints are unique, your strengths are unique to you. A wise and effective coach is able to understand, articulate, and communicate his strengths to his clients in a manner that defines his coaching roles.

How about you? Here are some questions that can help you consider your coaching roles:

- What are your God-given **talents?**

- What **knowledge** have you acquired or need to acquire that you can use to help the kind of clients God is calling you to serve?

- What **skills** have you developed or need to develop for the service of those who need your help?

- What **experiences** have you been through that will help you understand and relate to those God calls you to help?

About Roles

Your fit to your coaching roles is most critical. Your role defines your fit and your ability to respond to specific client needs.

As we discussed earlier, coaching can be defined in many ways and can take many different shapes and forms. Based on your clear understanding of your strengths it is your responsibility to define the roles you are prepared to play in a coaching relationship. In addition, it is your responsibility to direct your client to seek support or services that go beyond what you are prepared to offer.

The following are some questions that may help you discern your fit to coach:

- What draws you to coaching?

- What are you passionate about?

- What needs in the lives of people around you seem to interest you?

- What are you expert at or accomplished in?

- Are you a survivor of common life challenges?

- What kind of people or needs are you most attracted to?

- What have you experienced through success and failure that you can coach others through?

- Are you living a life that you want specific individuals or groups of people to emulate?

Note: For more on the development of your strengths and roles we recommend the Strengths Workshop resources available at http://integrity-plus.com/wp/sm/sw/ . You may get a free gift copy of our book, *The Strengths Workshop,* at our eStore at http://estore.strengthsworkshop.ca/?product=sw-ebook

About Listening and Questions

What do coaches do? What are the most important things coaches do? The answer is very simple; they **listen well and ask good questions.** Here Jesus gave us the model. He listened well and he asked a lot of penetrating questions.

Active listening is a skill. With a bit of good practice most of us can develop some active listening skills. Here some simple tips:

> "The primary function of the Coach is to understand. Not to solve, heal, make better, or be wise... The magic is that it is in that moment of understanding, the Client understands for himself, becomes more aware, and is then in a position to make better decisions and choices than he would have done anyway. This is how Coaching is profoundly simple and simply profound."
>
> **Myles Downey,** *Effective Coaching: Lessons from the Coaches' Coach*

- Try to listen in order to be able to repeat what you heard. Tell the client, "Let me tell you what I heard you say."

- Listen to the tone of voice and the emotions that hide behind the words.

- Listen prayerfully. Remember, Jesus is part of the conversation. Ask the Lord to reveal to you what He knows.

- Make strong eye contact.

- Let your body language communicate that you are listening.

- Remove all distractions so both you and your client can focus on each other.

- Remind the client that Jesus is part of the conversation. Ask your client to share what he just told you to Jesus in prayer.

Questions are more powerful than answers.

"Questions have the power to change lives. They can jump-start creativity, change our perspective, and empower us to believe in ourselves - push us to think things through or call us to action." [3] Asking the right questions and ensuring the client provides candid answers are the life-blood of a coaching session. This reveals the true skill of a Coach and the Client's readiness to change.

> Most people do not change because of what you tell them but much more by what you get them to tell you.

Questions encourage the Client to think. They help him move to a clearer state of awareness and uncover hidden solutions. In addition, questions help the Client understand the realities and the responsibilities associated with the issues or goals he faces. Questions are also a powerful tool to create focus, articulate assumptions, and qualify risks - as well as transitioning to actions that achieve desired outcomes.

Especially in Client-Directed Coaching, the Coach must rely heavily on open-ended questions that start with **how, what, why, who, or when**. The following are examples of the many types of questions a Coach might employ:

- **Revealing questions** encourage creativity and imagination. They invite the Client to think differently. Revealing questions seek to challenge limitations, beliefs, and established priorities.

    - Where are you right now in relation to…?
    - What do you like about where you are now…?
    - What don't you like about where you are now…?
    - What do you care about most deeply regarding…?
    - What are your unique strengths, skills, experiences…?
    - How did you feel about…?
    - What other pictures can you see when you think of….?
    - What values do you hold most dear…?
    - Who else can you consider for…?

- **Ownership questions** encourage the Client to take responsibility, be more proactive or define "**SMART**" goals and action steps.

    - What part are you playing in…?
    - What have you done that contributed to…?
    - What is it that you could have done differently…?
    - What do you want to do about…?
    - How can you change…?

- **Direct questions** seek focus, action, and/or accountability. When used wisely, these questions can help ensure that the coaching session provides the greatest benefit to the Client.

    - What progress did you make regarding…?
    - How will you communicate…?
    - What are you prepared to do next…?
    - When do you plan to…?
    - How can we be sure that you will…?
    - How can you share the change you are making to help others facing similar challenges?

About Motivation

Coaching, though very rewarding, is not easy. To be an effective coach you must clearly define what motivates you and keeps you invested in your client relationship. Much like most of the other helping professions, personal motivation must go well beyond the financial rewards and fees. Effective coaches are motivated by the improved wellbeing of their clients as well as the greater common good. The multiplied benefit is often seen in the ripple impact your coaching will have on the client's family life or work environment.

It is helpful that you keep track of progress and the impact of your coaching efforts. Encourage the client to communicate the change to you and others. Do you remember the note we received from our client, Kam? The most motivating tool we have found comes when a client sends you a note expressing the change he has made and the impact of your coaching on his life. Encourage the client to provide you with honest testimonies. These testimonies are not only for your motivation; more importantly it affirms the client in his commitment to change. Further, they serve to inspire others to seek help as well.

> **Here is one of the most powerful coaching tips we learned. When you have an opinion that you would like to share with your client, STOP, THIK and REPHRASE IT as a question.**
>
> **Allow the client a chance to articulate his or her own opinion as a response.**

Here again let us examine the model of Jesus Christ. While His desire was that "all may be saved" He understood that many will refuse his help and will not accept His teaching. As a matter of fact He was very selective in choosing His disciples. He dedicated the majority of His time and energy to a few who were willing and motivated to follow Him and be impacted by His ministry. In this way He gave us a model to ensure the right fit in a client/coach relationship. In dependence on Christ's Spirit the coach is responsible to make sure that the clients he coaches are compatible with his coaching purpose, style, and strengths.

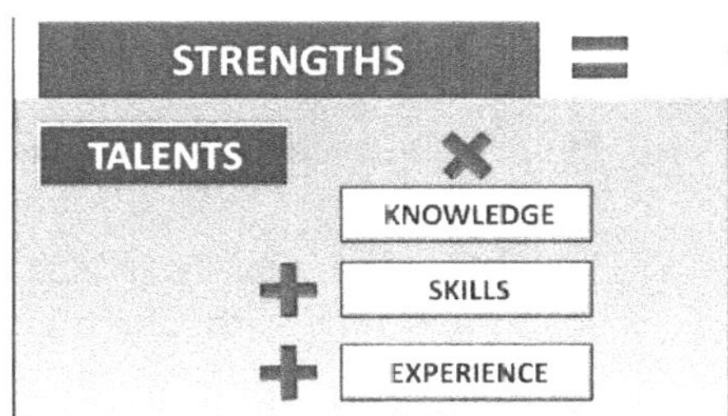

In coaching one of the first responsibilities is to discover your client's strengths and how they relate to his needs. As a coach you serve your clients out of who you are **but based on his strengths and what he wants to become.** Your ability to impact their lives is based on the strengths you bring but, more importantly, it is based on the strengths they possess. While it is critical that you know your strengths and motivation as a coach, it is even more critical that the client is able to know, understand, articulate, and communicate his own strengths and the needs that will cause him to change.

The same formula that we referenced to help you define your strengths can be used by your client to help him discover, articulate, and communicate his own strengths.

We live in a deficit based culture that constantly highlights our weaknesses. As a result, most of us focus on our weaknesses and all attempts to change and improve fail. Helping your client discover, articulate, and communicate his God given strengths could be the most affirming and encouraging outcome of a strengths based coaching relationship. Helping your client focus on his strengths will help him find his own avenues to change. You may offer your clients a free copy of the book, *The Strengths Workshop,* from our eStore at http://estore.strengthsworkshop.ca/?product=sw-ebook

About Needs

It has been said, *"You can take a horse to water but you cannot force it to drink."* As a coach you can never force people to change. All the coaching in the world will be a waste of time and energy unless the client has a genuine desire and willingness for change and wants to pay the price of change.

Clients will seek change as a result of **the Holy Spirit working in their life, a deep desire for something better** or **a life crisis that forces them to seek your help.** It is critical for the coach to discover if the desired change is internally driven or externally motivated. In other words, the client's desire must be out of genuine personal conviction. If the client indicates that he is seeking to change just to please someone else, the motivation will be short- lived and any coaching results will be temporary at best.

If your client comes to you as a result of a genuine desire for change and without external pressure of family or friends, your job as a coach is much easier and there are three simple steps that will help you launch a coaching relationship:

- First, make sure that the desired change is not in conflict with the declared will of God for all believers
- Help the client clearly articulate clear coaching objectives that are in harmony with Christ's desire to grant "abundant life"
- Along with the Spirit of Christ help your client set a reasonable plan towards achieving Christ centered objectives in a reasonable time manner

On the other hand, if the client comes to you as a result of a **critical life crisis,** emotional challenges and/or the demands of family, friends or managers, this presents a more complex situation that may require counseling or therapy before the coaching begins. It is critical that you discover this need and make sure your client seeks the appropriate help. Based on our experience, this is one the most common pitfalls in coaching relationships.

What motivates clients to seek coaching? The International Coaching Federation Global Survey lists the top 10 reasons for which people engage with a Coach: [2]

1. **Self-esteem/self-confidence**
2. **Work/life balance**
3. Career or business challenges or opportunities
4. Business management challenges
5. Relationships, either personal or business
6. Work performance
7. Interpersonal skills development
8. Communications skills development
9. Health and wellness
10. Team-effectiveness

---

[2] International Coaching Federation. Global Coaching Client study 2009. Page 4

 CHRIST CENTERED COACHING

Please note that the resources offered in **The Strengths Workshop** addresses the top two needs in the above list. As a coach, as early as possible, it is critical to identify the purpose or reason for which the client is seeking your help in the coaching relationship. If the client presents more than one reason it is important that you prioritize these reasons and deal with them one at a time.

About Confidentiality

Confidentiality is linked to trust in the coaching relationship. **Trust in a coaching relationship is like oxygen to the body.** The moment trust is removed the coaching relationship is compromised. The coach plays a vital role in ensuring the client has no doubt that what he shares remains confidential. He needs to be reminded that the purpose of a coaching relationship is primarily for the benefit of the Client.

The issue of confidentiality and trust is especially important when a manager or a leader is coaching his staff. To develop trust the manager has to put aside organizational and personal priorities in favor of the employee's best interests. It must be clearly understood that the Coach will maintain as much confidentiality as possible - within certain limits. These limits include legal constraints, ethical boundaries, and any risk of the Clients doing harm to themselves or others.

About Measurements

We value what we measure and we measure what we value. Since both Coach and Client are responsible for achieving effectiveness and success, they share the responsibility of measurement. If evaluation and measurements are ignored, this can lead to disappointment and misunderstanding which may have a long-term negative impact.

The effectiveness of the coaching sessions can be measured by the Client's progress in fulfilling their stated purpose, objective, and goals. The Progress Dashboard (see tools) is a helpful tool that provides a level of objectivity not only during the coaching relationship but even long after.

On the other hand, the Coach and Client can also rely on a qualitative perception by assessing how they feel about the effectiveness of each coaching session. For example, at the end of every session, both Coach and Client will indicate to what extent they agree with the following statement: **"This session was very effective".** Regular and candid session evaluation is a very effective tool in defining if the coaching relationship should continue or if it should be modified or terminated without any blame or guilt.

About Agreement

Should there be a coaching agreement? **Yes.** As with any high-value relationship, there are risks of miscommunication and misunderstanding. Verbal or written, a simple and clear coaching agreement seeks to mitigate misunderstandings and sets realistic expectations. The coaching agreement is part of the initiation exercises and should highlight:

1. **Purpose / Objectives:** Highlight the purpose and top two or three objectives that will be realized from this coaching relationship. It is preferable to use short-term objectives that can be realized in one to three months.

2. **Roles:** List the key roles the Coach is expected to play.

3. **Time Limited:** Indicate the estimated duration of this relationship. This should be linked to the objective time-horizon. Preference should be given to short-term agreements, which can be renewed with new objectives - if needed. The agreement should also state the frequency and duration of each coaching session. Also, indicate if conversations over phone or videophone are acceptable; these technologies may reduce travel and logistics costs.

4. **Progress Monitoring:** Indicate how progress will be monitored and success will be measured, as well as disengagement terms. This encourages accountability and appropriate use of resources.

5. **Price Based**: High value coaching has a high price. Rightly or wrongly, we often value services based on their cost. In order to realize the full potential coaching, **even when no fees are exchanged** (such as when managers coach staff or in the case of not-for-profit ministries), Clients need to be aware of the price paid by the Coach or others. **It is the responsibility of the Coach to frequently remind the Client of the cost** of misusing resources.

The Process

When we examine the story of creation or God's plan for salvation we see a process oriented God. The way God dealt with His people was intentional in everything He did. Jesus' life and ministry suggests that He valued intentional, disciplined relationships. Although different from one disciple to the other we can see that Jesus went about selecting His disciples and training them for ministry in a process oriented relationship.

- He prepared during forty days in the wilderness.

- He prayed before choosing His disciples.

- He met them where they were.

- He invited them into a relationship with Himself.

- He communicated the cost of the desired change.

- He set a clear understanding of the objectives.

- He spent much time with them.

- He used parables, illustrations, and a language they could understand.

- He encouraged them to follow His example.

Coaching is a high value relationship that often has a long-term impact. For this reason it should be taken seriously by both coach and client. The best clients are prepared clients.

A coaching relationship starts in a variety of format. The story we shared earlier about our meeting with Kam illustrates casual encounters that reveal some needs that you can respond to as a coach. At other times it may be a referral from a pastor or a friend.

As a purpose

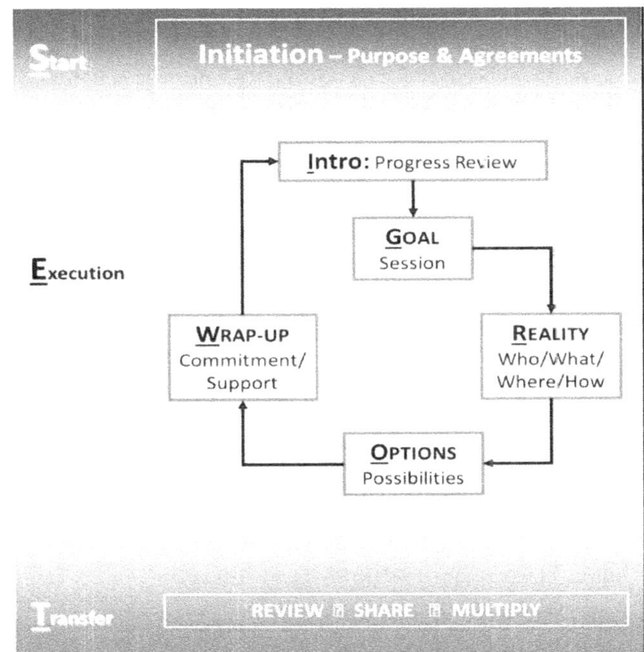

driven relationship, once you go beyond the informal casual introductions you, as the Coach, must set clear expectations of a disciplined process oriented relationship. The attached diagram and descriptions offer a topical framework of a coaching process that we have used with our clients. We used to call it Self or Client Directed Coaching because the client directs the coaching objectives and the goals for each coaching meeting while the coach controls the process. From a Christian perspective we like to refer to this process as Christ Centered Coaching.

SET (**S**tart, **E**xecution, and **T**ransfer), illustrated in the attached diagram, highlights the elements that contribute to a successful and transferable coaching relationship.

Start: The beginning of a relationship sets the stage for its success or failure. An initiation meeting is where needs are uncovered and objectives are communicated. As soon as possible, the Coach and Client must agree on confidentiality, meeting frequency, and how long the coaching relationship will last. It is helpful to agree on the key tools or resources that will be used to enhance the coaching process. It is in this stage that discovery and communication tools can be very helpful. Later, we will discuss some specific tools that we find helpful in our work.

Execution: This is the stage where the rubber hits the road. This repeated process is at the heart of a Coaching relationship. It is a series of purpose-driven conversations or sessions that use the model: "**I   G R O W**". GROW is the most widely adapted coaching model. The Progress Dashboard, presented later, is a simple low-overhead tool that provides structure and support for each coaching conversation.

> **I**ntro: A review of progress and challenges is a valuable introduction to every coaching session. With caring, accountability, and support, the Client is encouraged to persevere in reaching agreed-upon objectives.

> **G**oal: It is the responsibility of the Client to articulate clear goals for the coaching session. Focusing on goals that are **SMART** (**S**pecific, **M**easurable, **A**ttainable, **R**elevant, and **T**ime dependent) is critical to successful Coaching conversations.

> **R**eality: Here, the Coach guides the Client in painting a **true picture** of the reality he faces. Use open-ended **revealing questions** such as: "**What's** the real problem with...?", "**Who** else is involved in...?", "**What** happens if..?", "**How** do you feel about...?", and "**Where** would you...?" This technique ignites the Client's creativity. Understanding arises out of his own internal resources, which may not have otherwise occurred.

> **O**ptions: As the Client uncovers the reality of issues, people, feelings, opportunities, and obstacles, many solutions and opportunities will

emerge. With skillful understanding, the most appropriate options will become clear. Now the Client is ready to make commitments and take action. Here the coach will use **ownership questions** to help the client see what he or she can do. Such as "What can you consider ..." "What is likely to happen if ..." "Who you should see to..." What would happen if you ..." "What steps can you take to ..."

> **W**rap up: As the Client defines his action-plans, and commits to timely execution; the Coach will play an encouraging and supportive role. Even in Client-Directed Coaching, where a Coach does not assume much authority, the Coach must exercise (and the Client must accept) **supportive accountability**. This is essential. Here the coach will use **direct questions** to help the client move to committed action plans. Such as "What are you prepared to do ..." "Which of these options will you take ..." "When will you..." "How will you do ..."

Transfer: At certain points in the Coaching relationship, it is helpful for the Coach and Client to review and highlight the outcomes of their efforts, and the lessons learned. Sharing success, whenever possible or appropriate, affirms the Client's commitment to ongoing improvement. Skills-transfer is a powerful way to enforce the lessons learned. **"If you want to be a master of an art, Coach it"**. It is highly recommended that the Client finds teachable people that he/she can help by modeling the skills observed in the Coaching relationship. This has a **multiplying benefit** for all concerned. In other words, as early as possible, you as a coach should encourage your client to coach others as well. Remember *"As iron sharpens iron, so one man sharpens another."* Nothing will affirm your client in what he learned as much as the benefit he will gain from coaching others.

I GROW Questions

The following table presents a set of questions mapped to the **I GROW** model.

I GROW: Coaching Questions

Initiation	• **How are you?** Physically → Emotionally → Financially → Spiritually / Character → * **Progress & Challenges**
Goal	• **How Can I help you today?** Specific → Measurable → Attainable → Relevant → Time Dependent

<table>
<tr><td>R
E
A
L
I
T
Y</td><td>

UNCOVERING THE REAL ISSUES: Ask revealing questions:

- **The past:** What led to this? Can you give me the background? What else caused this?
- **The future:** Where will this lead to? What change do you want and why?
- **Patterns:** How often does this happen? Do you see a pattern in here?
- **Emotions:** How do you feel about that? How do others feel?
- **Other viewpoints:** How do you think others see this? If you were in their place how...?
- **Concrete:** Can you give me a specific example of...? What exactly did you/they say and do?
- **Values:** What values do you hold dear? What do you believe about...?
- **Heart of the matter:** What is the real issue/ concern and why?

</td></tr>
<tr><td>O
P
T
I
O
N
S</td><td>

EMPOWERMENT: Ask ownership questions

- **Five options:** What are five options to..., what else...?
- **The past:** What have you done in the past that worked in similar...?
- **Obstacles:** What is stopping you from...? What do you need that you do not have to...?
- **Ideal future:** What would the future state look like? # of months from now how would it look...?
- **Work backward:** What needs to happen? What must you change...? Would you walk me through the process? Can you imagine things changing …?
- **Outside the box:** Can you think of yourself as a change agent? What if...? What beliefs drive you to...?

</td></tr>
<tr><td>W
R
A
P

U
P</td><td>

COULD do → WANT to do → WILL do. Ask direct questions.

- **Options:** Which of these options do you favour and why?
- **Could:** What could you do to change...?
- **Want:** What do you want to do and WHY?
- **Will:** What will you do? Would you give me the steps...? Can we role play this...?
- **Insurance:** How can you be sure you will...? What would happen if...? Do you need accountability?   **To be sure:**
    - **Clarity:** How can we make sure this is very clear?
    - **Datebook:** When will you do this? Can you put in your calendar?
    - **Commitment:** How can we be sure you will...?
    - **Deadline:** What is the latest time frame?
- **Progress reporting:** Will you let me know that...?   Will you call me if you are not able to...?

</td></tr>
</table>

    CHRIST CENTERED COACHING

The Tools

Like any profession or trade effective coaching relies on tools. Coaching tools serve to help your client discover and apply the truth. They help your client think and communicate truth. Jesus said, *"…you will know the truth, and the truth will set you free." John 8:32.* Reaching a clear understanding of truth liberates the client and unlocks the door to most of our life challenges.

While we are reluctant to refer to the Bible as a tool, The Bible is the most comprehensive coaching manual. Paul tells his disciple Timothy that, *"all scripture is given by inspiration of God, and is profitable for doctrine, for reproof, for correction, for instruction in righteousness." 2 Timothy 3:16.*

Jesus gave us a model. He referred to the scriptures in many of His teaching and coaching relationships. In addition, Jesus gives a good model in the use of illustrations, stories, and parables as teaching and coaching tools. In her book, *Jesus, Life Coach*, Laurie Beth Jones describes how Jesus, by His life and teaching, provided a coaching resource in response to most of our life questions.

Tools can be as simple as our "How are you gauge" we illustrated in Baha's first conversation with Kam. On the other end of the spectrum, there are tools that require study and have financial costs associated with them.

Coaches employ different tools, resources, or exercises to support the roles they play and the type of clients they best serve. More importantly, tools must fit the purpose of the Coaching relationship. We believe that tools are most effective when they are administered by the Client, and can be used independently of the Coach long after the end of the coaching relationship. These tools become life-long exercises.

In Client-Directed Coaching, exercises serve as thinking and communication templates. They are used primarily for the benefit of the Client to help him communicate his thoughts and feelings. These exercises will increase the Coach's effectiveness.

Search the web or read coaching books and you will find a vast inventory of coaching tools. Most coaching tools can be broken into two categories:

- **Discovery and initiation tools:** The first nine exercises are designed to facilitate the Client's self-discovery and help define the foundations on which you can create coaching objectives and a coaching plan.

- **Progress tools:** The Progress Dashboard is a simple, low overhead, discussion tool that provides some structure, outline or agenda for each coaching conversation. It also helps the Client own his progress and direct coaching priorities.

Note:

The appendix of this booklet presents an execution process and a set of tools designed specifically for Strengths Coaching. These include eight discovery and initiation exercises and more than 30 progress related exercises. Many of these exercises can be modified and used for other than Strengths coaching. The following discovery and initiation exercises are highly transferable.

1. How Are You?

The attached image is a simple business card size tool that I keep in my wallet and use very often. I use it to start a conversation with friends, clients, and even strangers. I simple say **"Would you like to tell me how you really feel physically, emotionally, financially and or spiritually?"** In the appendix you will find a longer related exercise.

How Are You?

Physically   Financially

Emotionally   Spiritually

This exercise goes several steps beyond the simple "How are you gauge." By responding to a set of 12 statements, the purpose of this exercise is to help your Client communicate how he feels: physically, emotionally, financially, and spiritually. It also sets the stage for the improvements he desires. As a Coach, your priority is to help your Client move from his present state to a better one. This exercise seeks to insert a level of objectivity into the coaching session. It serves as a bit of self-diagnosis by which the Client can explain how he feels on a range of 1 – 5. It is also helpful to indicate the desired change or target. As you will see in the last exercise, the summary of this survey also provides you with a language to use in every coaching session that follows.

2. Defining Core Values

The purpose of this exercise is to help your Client define what is truly important in his life. Whether we know them or not - even if we cannot articulate them - our core values drive our life. Our core values are what we value more than anything else. These are the things, issues, or relationships that we are not willing to compromise. Someone once said, "They are the values that we are even willing to die for."

Core values are the bedrock of life - on which we build our future priorities, our direction, and any desired changes. Regretfully we seldom define them or communicate them. Since coaching is a purpose-driven relationship, it is wise to ensure that the Client's core values are articulated and communicated.

3. Roles - Love-Hate Inventory

This exercise seeks to help your Client think and prioritize his most important life roles. On the stage of life, we are often given titles or professional designations. Embedded in each of these titles are many roles. Some of these are roles we love and some are roles we hate. The roles we love often rely on our most dominant character strengths. Again, the objective is to help the Client see and communicate the roles where he can focus - to bring about the greatest beneficial changes.

Going further as we play our many life roles, we are given responsibilities and tasks to fulfill. Apart from the impact of relationships, and the people engaged in these activities, what we love and hate are good indicators of where we are most likely to change and where we face our greatest challenges. For this reason, this self-awareness exercise can be a helpful coaching tool. The purpose is to help the Client see the relationships between the strengths, roles, responsibilities, and activities that he loves or hates.

4. Love Language

The demands of life make withdrawals from your emotional bank account. Those who are important to you make deposits into your emotional bank accounts. Those who are close to you have a unique ability to energize you and build you up emotionally.

In his bestselling book, *The Five Love Languages,*4 Dr. Gary Chapman deals with this concept of filling our emotional bank accounts. Deposits into your emotional bank account come in the form of receiving love. He suggests that using the right love language is the best tool for that currency exchange.

As a coach, understanding the five love languages and the love language of your Client will enhance your coaching relationship. Further, it will help you understand how your client is motivated and how the important people in his life can help him move towards the desired change. You should encourage your client to take the Five Love Languages survey at http://www.5lovelanguages.com/

5. Coaching Objectives

This exercise helps your Client focus on why he needs your help, and how to achieve the results he seeks. Objectives are statements of faith, which highlight what the Client wishes to achieve from the coaching experience. These objectives will also help the Coach gauge his ability to meet the Client's needs.

Using short, simple sentences, the Client should list two or three objectives that paint a picture of what he would like to achieve in their coaching sessions. The Client should list why each of these objectives is important to him.

6. Coach's Role

Ensuring a good fit is the purpose of this exercise. Coaching is not a one-size-fits-all activity; as a Coach, you cannot be all things to all people. Successful Coaches ensure that their own strengths and styles are a good match for the Client's needs. As stated earlier, Coaches can play many roles. This exercise has two parts:

- **First,** the Coach, based on his strengths and style, has a responsibility to define a few roles he is willing to consider playing or indicate where he wants to focus his energies and his practice.
- **Second,** through candid dialog, the Client can prioritize these roles and ensure that they are compatible with his needs and objectives.

The following are a sample of common coaching roles:

- **Accountability source:** To act in a way that encourages specific behavior towards the fulfillment of agreed-upon objectives and or commitments
- **Advisor:** To provide advice on a clearly articulated question, or questions, based on one's specific area of knowledge skills or experience

  Advisor: (alternate) to provide or find educated opinions on specific matters, or answers to specific questions. Or, recommend resources or appropriate course of action
- **Catalyst:** To act as an agent that provokes or speeds a significant change or action
- **Counselor:** To provide guidance, solutions, or a professional opinion, relating to a personal, social, or psychological problem or need
- **Empathizer:** To share feelings in a time of need, emotional hurt, or stress
- **Recourse:** To provide help in a difficult situation, by providing assistance or tangible resources to meet special needs
- **Sounding board:** To provide honest reactions to ideas, opinions, or points of view to help clarify a Client's effectiveness or application

7. Progress Dashboard

The purpose of this template is to provide a process that directs each coaching conversation. As we described earlier, in a Client-Directed Coaching relationship, the Client directs the coaching objectives and the Coach directs the process. This tool provides each coaching session with a structure and a communication template. **Prepared by the**

Client, this template offers him the opportunity to reflect and document his progress and challenges. It is also a way to communicate to the Coach where to best invest the limited time of each coaching session.

This template provides a simple five-part coaching process illustrated in the earlier sections:

1. **The Introduction** helps the Client respond to the important **"How are you"** question. How the Client feels sets the tone and priorities of a caring relationship. To lend a bit of objectivity, the Client is encouraged to indicate, on a scale of 1 – 5, how he feels: physically, emotionally, financially and spiritually. Please note that this is a summary of the input provided in the first exercise.

    To help provide continuity from one session to the next, the Client is encouraged to record and share their accomplishments since the last session, as well as any challenges or obstacles encountered. Depending on what is shared and the time available, the Coach may use this as springboard for further discussion.

    Goal setting is important. Coaching time is limited. Goal setting ensures that the Client defines what he would like to achieve by the end of the coaching session.

2. **Coaching discussion notes** help the Client and the Coach remember important and helpful thoughts for follow-up, support, and accountability.

    - **Reality discussion** creates and records clear understanding of the issue at hand.

    - **Options discussion** seeks to help narrow down the choices available, and the impact of each, before agreeing on the best action-plan.

    - **Wrapping up the coaching session** is an agreement on the specific actions the Client is prepared to take. The Coach may ask the Client question like these:

        - So - what would you like to do?
        - Is this what you commit to do?
        - When do you expect to do…?
        - How will I know you have done it?

STRENGTHS COACHING

A Supplement to Christ Centered Coaching

This supplement provides a process and a toolset to help you develop your God given **strengths** by integrating them into your **roles, relationships, and life plans**. This is a **six step process.** You may tailor these coaching tools to your needs as you choose from 40 thinking exercises. To help you record and communicate your thoughts and action plans with each exercise you will find easy to **use templates**.

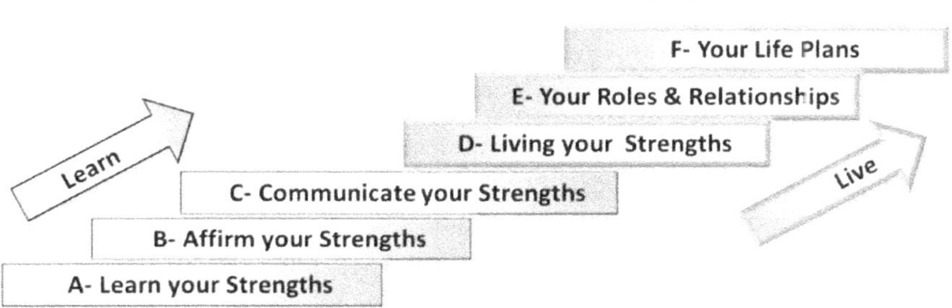

As illustrated in this supplement we provide you with a **two phase Strengths Coaching process.** Each phase has three steps:

1. **Learn your Strengths.** Your identity is not based on what you do but much more on who you are. As you become intimately aware of your top strengths you can manage your lowest strengths and compensate for your lesser strengths. By your life experiences and the affirmation of your important relationships you will appropriate your God given strengths.

2. **Living your Strengths.** Your life callings are not defined by your title, a to-do list or the expectations of others, but by the important roles you are called to play. Living your strengths is investing and applying your strengths to your important life roles. This will improve your effectiveness, enhance your relationships, and lead to more work-life balance.

Keep Christ at the center. At the beginning of each step pray for **God's guidance.** At the end of each step **seek God's wisdom** as you define your application oriented focus and action plan.

For those who wish to help others develop their God given strengths this supplement provides a toolbox that they can edit and use to develop their own coaching ministry.

INTRODUCTION

Do you want to prioritize your life roles and relationships as you develop and grow your God given strengths? If you answered yes, please read on.

Your strengths are like your muscles; as you exercise them they develop, serve you, and bring glory to the one who gave them to you. At the start, commit to a disciplined plan. Be ready to invest the time and interest in the exercises provided in this process.

While you may take this process by yourself, the support of a friend or a coach will be most helpful. Coaches ask questions to help you to think and discover answers for yourself. We have structured this paper to be a transferable coaching tool. Through its questions **I will act as your coach.** I will be asking you some coaching questions followed by templates or a space for your answers.

Each of the six steps has a unique function. We encouraged you to see this as a process fulfilling your coaching objectives. While we encourage you to follow the six steps in sequence, you have the option to skip some exercises or questions. Some questions will take little time while others may require more thinking.

One simple advice: avoid being too analytical. Your first impression is often the most important. The last exercise in each step we ask you to reflect and record the most important thing you learned from that step, the application from what you learned, and the way that this relates to your coaching objective. Further, you are encouraged to share this with your friend or coach.

In this paper, we assume that you have taken the **Strengths Workshop.** If not, we encourage you to go to the self-study Strengths Workshop at http://integrity-plus.com/wp/sm/sp/. There you will find resources to help you discover your strengths and a process to help you discern your life callings

Please note:

- At http://integrity-plus.com/Data/Templates/StrengthsDev.docx download an MS Word copy of this supplement. Make this a living document that you can update as you know more about your strengths and as your life roles change.

- As a transferable coaching tool, this is a supplement to the Christ Centered Coaching booklet. Get a free gift copy at http://estore.strengthsworkshop.ca/product/coach-2.

- The last section includes additional tools to help you coach others and develop your coaching practice. **Feel free to adapt it to your coaching needs.**

     Strengths Coaching Process and Tools

Initiation

As your coach, I do not see myself as someone who knows how to do life better than you; rather I see myself as someone who wants to see you do life better than you thought you could. Any coaching process starts with initiation or some self-discovery questions. These questions will also help me know you and learn how I can support you in reaching your coaching objectives. Once you have completed these discovery exercises, please share them with me as your coach.

1. How are you?

Each coaching conversation will start with this familiar question. As your coach, because I care I want to know more than the habitual "I am fine." This is a simple assessment and discussion tool. Through the coaching process our goal is to improve your overall wellbeing. These scores can be used to track progress or coaching success. **Please complete all the Gray cells.**

To what extent do you agree with the following statements? (copy and paste **X** for your response)	I TOTALLY Agree ↔ Disagree				
A. Physical					
1. My health is at an optimum state.	5	4	3	2	1
2. I sleep very well.	5	4	3	2	1
Average Physical Score	(total divided by 2)				
B. Emotional					
3. My family life is very fulfilling and rewarding.	5	4	3	2	1
4. My relationships with my co-workers are collaborative and supportive.	5	4	3	2	1
5. I love my work. At work I feel equipped and empowered to regularly be my best and do what I am best at doing.	5	4	3	2	1
6. My work-life is totally balanced.	5	4	3	2	1
Average Physical Score	(total divided by 4)				
C. Financial And Development					
7. My financial affairs are totally under control.	5	4	3	2	1
8. I feel well rewarded for the work I do.	5	4	3	2	1
9. My personal growth and development plans support my need for financial stability and/or future objectives.	5	4	3	2	1
Average Physical Score	(total divided by 3)				
D. Spiritual					
10. My values are clear and are supported by my spiritual faith and beliefs.	5	4	3	2	1
11. I am fully aware of my character strengths and weaknesses.	5	4	3	2	1
12. My family, friends, and co-workers support my values and priorities.	5	4	3	2	1
Average Physical Score	(total divided by 3)				

Desired Change: If things improve, what would your rating be? **Copy and paste C beside your desired score.**

- **As your coach** I will compare the progress dashboard **"How are you?"** score for possible improvements.

Strengths Coaching Process and Tools

Coach Tony Stoltzfus writes, **"Values are the bedrock of behaviors. They define what is important to us, they form the framework we use for making decisions, and they are the driving force behind our work and our passions."** Core values are like the rudder that steers the ship to keep it on course.

This five-step exercise helps you start a process of writing your core values and sharing them with others:

1. Using the list below select List key descriptive words that mean the most to you. Which words **you are most passionate about** or care about the most? Placing an **A** besides these words. Add more words as needed. Most likely you will start with a fairly long list. That is OK.

2. Narrow your list by placing **B** beside any word that represents something that is unique about you and/or you are presently engaged in or form a significant part of your present or desired work or personal life. This is your **B** list.

☐ Accomplishments	☐ Emotion	☐ Integrity	☐ Recognition
☐ Accountability	☐ Enthusiasm	☐ Intimacy	☐ Reflection
☐ Achievement	☐ Entrepreneur ship	☐ Investment	☐ Relationship
☐ Advancement	☐ Evangelism	☐ Knowledge	☐ Renewal
☐ Adventure	☐ Excellence	☐ Leadership	☐ Responsibility
☐ Artistic	☐ Exploration	☐ Legacy	☐ Romance
☐ Authenticity	☐ Family	☐ Lifelong learning	☐ Sacrifice
☐ Beauty	☐ Finances	☐ Love	☐ Security
☐ Knowledgeable	☐ Flexibility	☐ Marriage	☐ Service
☐ Being known	☐ Focus	☐ Mastery	☐ Sincerity
☐ Belonging	☐ Follow through	☐ Meaning	☐ Spiritual life
☐ Benevolence	☐ Freedom	☐ Motivation	☐ Spontaneity
☐ Building	☐ Friendship	☐ Movement	☐ Stability
☐ Caring	☐ Frugality	☐ Nature	☐ Starting things
☐ Change	☐ Fun	☐ New challenges	☐ Stewardship
☐ Character	☐ Generosity	☐ Nurture	☐ Strategy
☐ Commitment	☐ Gentleness	☐ Opportunity	☐ Strength
☐ Communication	☐ Governance	☐ Policy	☐ Success
☐ Community	☐ Harmony	☐ Perfection	☐ Team
☐ Compassion	☐ Healing	☐ Passionate pursuit	☐ Thoughtfulness
☐ Competence	☐ Health	☐ Peace	☐ Travel
☐ Concern	☐ Heritage	☐ Planning	☐ Truth
☐ Creativity	☐ Honesty	☐ Practicality	☐ Volunteering
☐ Depth	☐ Honor	☐ Precision	☐ World Issues
☐ Devotion	☐ Hospitality	☐ Principles	☐ Worship
☐ Directness	☐ Identity	☐ Progress	☐ Add more
☐ Diversity	☐ Influence	☐ Purpose	☐ Add more
☐ Duty	☐ Inspiration	☐ Rationality	☐ Add more
☐ Efficiency	☐ Integration	☐ Reaching out	

3. Narrow your (**B**) list by listing your top **five core values** in order of priority below:

1.	2.	3.	4.	5.

3. *What roles do you love or hate?*

You have many **responsibilities** where you are accountable and are called on to play many roles. These are areas that impact your life and goals. List your important personal and work life responsibilities.
- Indicate to what degree you love or hate each. Mark an ✕ for your answer.
- What is the % of time you give to each of your most important roles

% of Time	Roles and Responsibilities. You may also include major activities	I STRONGLEY Love ←←←←←→→→→→Hate				
		5	4	3	2	1
		5	4	3	2	1
		5	4	3	2	1
		5	4	3	2	1
		5	4	3	2	1
		5	4	3	2	1
		5	4	3	2	1
		5	4	3	2	1
		5	4	3	2	1
		5	4	3	2	1
		5	4	3	2	1
		5	4	3	2	1
		5	4	3	2	1
		5	4	3	2	1
		5	4	3	2	1
		5	4	3	2	1
		5	4	3	2	1
		5	4	3	2	1

Strengths Coaching Process and Tools

4. What is your favorite love language?

As your coach I would like to encourage you and affirm you in your progress. We all like to be affirmed and encouraged in our unique way. One of the best resources on this subject is the Five Love Language. Finding your love language can help you in many aspects of your life. Please take a short survey at http://www.5lovelanguages.com/ and then enter your Love Language Scores in the table below.

Acts of Service		Physical Touch		Quality Time	
Receiving Gifts		Words of Affirmation			

5. What are your coaching objectives?

Just like developing muscles, you need objectives that respond to real life needs that call for real change. Prayerfully identify areas of your life, roles or relationships where developing your Strengths can help you grow or improve. List two coaching objectives and the reasons why these are important. **Start every objective with a verb.**

Objectives – Desired Change	Need or reason for Importance
1.	
2.	

It was wisely said that a picture is worth a thousand words. Watch this video **https://www.youtube.com/watch?v=4vl6wCiUZYc.** You may not be an artist, I am sure you can scribble, sketch and paint stick figures. On a separate page draw a sketch or illustration of your life, roles, relationships or the change you like to see.

6. *What is your development plan?*

The following pages provide a **six step** Strengths Coaching plan. Each step includes around five thinking exercises. Just like in seeking physical fitness, your progress is directly related to how often you exercise and how much time you invest exercising. This is totally up to you. While you have freedom in the exercises you chose, you should **follow the six steps outlined**. Set realistic expectations based on the amount of time you can afford to spend. Here are some thoughts to guide your planning:

- Try to cover steps one to five in **5 – 10 weeks. Dedicate 2–4 hours** for exercising per week. These are thinking exercises. Some exercises will take longer than other. It is natural that some exercises will appeal to you more than others. Whatever you do, try to make this enjoyable.

- The time required for Step 6, "**your development project**", will depend on the project scope and complexity. Preference should be given to simpler projects requiring less time.

- Meeting with your coach should be weekly or biweekly. Plan to spend 60–90 minutes for each coaching visit. For maximum benefit, plan 15–30 minutes after every coaching visit to reflect on what you discussed and what you plan to do.

Question	Answer: Be as specific.
• How much time per week will you invest in your strengths development?	
• When? Set a weekly rhyme. State week days and time.	
• Who will support you or coach you in fulfilling your plan? When or how are you going to meet?	

7. What are my coaching roles?

As your coach, I can play many roles. In the table below I have listed four common coaching roles. Consider your personality, needs and coaching objectives. Prioritize the roles you want me to play from 1–4. **(1 most important – 4 least important)**

Priority 1 - 4	Role
•	**Accountability source:** To act in a way that encourages specific behavior toward the fulfillment of agreed upon objectives and or commitments
•	**Advisor:** To provide or find educated opinions on specific matters or answers to specific questions or to recommend an appropriate course of action
•	**Catalyst:** To act as an agent that provokes or speeds significant change or action
•	**Sounding board:** To provide honest reactions to ideas, opinions, or points of view to help you clarify their effectiveness or application

8. How do we measure your progress?

We measure what we value. Your progress is critical to our continued relationship. This is why I use a tool we call the progress dashboard. Each coaching session is a goal oriented conversation that seeks to move you closer to the desired objective. To ensure that each session brings the greatest value, we modified a very popular coaching process with the acronym **"IGROW"**:

- **I**nitiation and progress review is the start of each coaching session. This is the time to celebrate achievements and **review issues and challenges**. Here you will be expected to record the best you have learned and what change you desire to see because of what you have learned.

- **G**oals set at the beginning of each coaching session will help us keep our focus and deliver results.

- **R**eality discussions seek to bring candid clarity to the real issues you need to face.

- **O**ptions review will help you examine and narrow down the directions you can take.

- **W**rapping up each coaching session by agreeing on **S**pecific, **M**easurable, **A**ttainable, **R**elevant, and **T**ime dependent activities. This will help you move forward to fulfilling the desired objectives.

1. Download a blank copy of this dashboard from: http://integrity-plus.com/Data/Templates/StrengthsDev.docx

2. Before each coaching session, complete the **Initiation & Goal** parts of this template and e-mail your Progress Dashboard to your coach at least 24 hours before your session. This will give him/her time to prepare for your coaching meeting. The remaining three parts (R.O.W) provide a space to note the results of your coaching conversation.

Note:

- During this process you will need some resources. Please collect them and become familiar with them:

  ✓ **Your Strengthsfinder2.0** reports at https://www.GallupStrengthCenter.com/SignIn/en-US/Index

- Strengths Insights Report
- Ideas for Actions
- Examples for Strengths

  ✓ Discovering Your Lowest Five Strengths http://integrity-plus.com/SM/Notes/LS-SF2.0-Alt.pdf
  ✓ The Strengths Workshop Exercise Book. http://estore.strengthsworkshop.ca/product/sw-ebook
  ✓ Your Spiritual Gifts Inventory. See http://www.spiritualgiftstest.com/test/adult
  ✓ The Going Deeper resources available at http://estore.strengthsworkshop.ca/welcome/gd

Where you see this book icon, it will refer to content in the **Strengths Workshop Book**.

Strengths Coaching Process and Tools

A. *Learn Your Strengths*

According to the parable of the talents in Matthew 25, you have a God given responsibility to know your strengths. Knowing your strengths is an intentional process. In the process of knowing your strengths you must be able to describe your top five strengths, know your weaknesses or

> Pray: "Lord, help me learn the truth about the strengths you gave me."

lowest strengths so you can manage them or avoid their pitfalls, and discern your lesser strengths so you can leverage them when you need them. With this knowledge, you will move to affirm and appropriate your strengths so you can communicate them with authenticity.

1. How do you describe your strengths?

Go to your StrengthsFinder2.0 **Strengths insight report.** Read it, highlighting every adjective, statement and term that reflects your character traits or leads you to say **"that's me"**. In the space below, summarize these adjectives in few sentences. Where possible use the term **"I am…"**

Do this for each of your five Strengths themes. Read what you wrote out loud as if you are reading to a friend or family member. **Update this as you learn more about your strengths.**

For an example of this go to the Going deeper videos http://estore.strengthsworkshop.ca/welcome/gd. There you will find short one minute video clips for each of the 34 strengths themes.

First Theme	
I am …	

<table>
<tr><td>Second Theme</td><td></td></tr>
</table>

I am …

<table>
<tr><td>Third Theme</td><td></td></tr>
</table>

I am …

<table>
<tr><td>Fourth Theme</td><td></td></tr>
</table>

I am …

<table>
<tr><td>Fifth Theme</td><td></td></tr>
</table>

I am …

The shadow side of your strengths is when strength becomes a cause for stress or pain to you or others. We all face the risk of the shadow side of our strengths. Just as you can describe your strengths using adjectives you can describe the shadow side of your strengths using adjectives.

 *Refer to Exercise 10 in the Strengths Workshop book.*

In the space below, list key adjectives or terms that describe the shadow side of each of your top 5 strengths themes. Read what you wrote out loud as if you are reading to a friend or family member. **Update this as you learn more about the shadow side of your strengths.**

First Theme	
I have a risk of being …	

Second Theme	
I have a risk of being …	

Third Theme	

I have a risk of being ...

Fourth Theme	

I have a risk of being ...

Fifth Theme	

I have a risk of being ...

3. *How do you describe your lowest Strengths?*

Go to http://integrity-plus.com/SM/Notes/LS-SF2.0-Alt.pdf. Download a
document with instructions on how to discover your lowest strengths.
Read the one paragraph full description related to each of your lowest
Strengths. Highlight every adjective and statement that is contrary to
your character traits or leads you to say **"that is NOT me"**. In the
space below, summarize what you highlighted. Where possible use the
term **"I am not ..."** These are the Strengths themes that you need to
avoid.

Read what you wrote out loud as if you are reading to a friend or family
member. **Update this as you learn more about your lowest
strengths.**

Theme 30	
I am not ...	

Theme 31	
I am not ...	

Strengths Coaching Process and Tools

<table>
<tr><td>Theme 32</td><td></td></tr>
<tr><td colspan="2">I am not …</td></tr>
<tr><td>Theme 33</td><td></td></tr>
<tr><td colspan="2">I am not …</td></tr>
<tr><td>Theme 34</td><td></td></tr>
<tr><td colspan="2">I am not …</td></tr>
</table>

4. *Which of your lesser Strengths can you use?*

Your lesser strengths are the Strengths Themes below your top 5. It is often helpful to leverage these strengths in defining your roles and relationships. Follow the same process you used to define your lowest strengths. This time, seek to find and highlight statements that describe you or makes you say, **"That's me"** or **"that could be me."** Complete the table below.

Read what you wrote out loud as if you are reading to a friend or family member. **Update this as you learn more about your lesser strengths.**

Theme 6	
I could be …	

Theme 7	
I could be …	

Strengths Coaching Process and Tools

Theme 8	
I could be …	

Theme 9	
I could be …	

Theme 10	
I could be …	

Prayerfully, ask **God** to help you define the best you have learned through the "Know your Strengths" steps? What changes would you like to do as a result? **How does this relate to your coaching objectives?**

The Best I Learned	Desired Change or Actions

- **For your Coach,** include this summary in your progress dashboard and send it to your coach before your next coaching session.

B. AFFIRM YOUR STRENGTHS

There are many ways to help you affirm and own your strengths. This includes your past and present experiences, the roles you played with joy, the feedback of your important people, and how you complement the strengths of your important people.

6. How does experience affirm your Strengths?

In the following table, divide your life into logical time segments. Say every 10 years. For each period recall events, experiences, or times when you felt strong, empowered, and fulfilled. List rewarding accomplishments that brought you joy and a sense of purpose. These events or moments often reflect times when you used your strengths. List the strengths you may have used.

Life Period	Highlights, events, moments, or experiences when you felt strong or fulfilled	Possible Strengths Used

7. What roles affirm your strengths?

Examine the list you created in the previous exercise. Identify significant or roles you played in these events or experiences. These roles often reflect times when you used your strengths. In the table below describe the roles you played. Relate this to the strengths you may have used.

Highlights roles, when you felt strong or fulfilled	Possible Strengths

For more on roles see Section C in the Strengths Workshop book and related appendix.

Strengths Coaching Process and Tools

8. What people affirm your Strengths?

In exercise 1, you wrote your own description for each of your top 5 strengths. Identify 3 people who know you well. Read your strengths descriptions to each of them. Ask them for their feedback or how they see these traits reflected in you. Note their comments or observations.

Strengths	1st Person	2nd Person	3rd Person

9. How important people affirm your strengths

Important people partner and collaborate with you in life roles and responsibilities. They have similar life purposes but may have **different strengths and/or different roles**. Understanding their differences will affirm you in understanding your own strengths and roles.

List at least 3 important people and explain how their strengths and roles compliment your strengths and roles. **Share what you learned with these important people.**

Name	Complementary Strengths and Roles

For more on the important people impact, reference Section D in the Strengths Workshop book.

Prayerfully, ask God to help you define the best you have learned through the **"Affirm your Strengths"** steps? What changes would you like to do as a result? **How does this relate to your coaching objectives?**

The Best I Learned	Desired Change or Actions

- **For your Coach,** include this summary in your progress dashboard and send it to your coach before your next coaching session.

C. COMMUNICATE YOUR STRENGTHS

If you do not communicate your strengths clearly and accurately, others will assume them for you. With this, you risk the possibility of being cast into wrong roles or given unrealistic responsibilities and expectations.

> **Pray: "Lord, help me communicate the truth about my strengths."**

11. What is your Strengths profile?

Your strengths profile is your strengths inventory list. It is a brief listing that describes each of your strengths. For each strength list:

- Your **talents** using adjectives
- Your **competencies** (knowledge + skills + experience)
- Your **shadow.** The risks you fear as a result of overusing your strengths

Strengths	Talents: I am ...	Competencies: I bring ...	Shadow: I fear ...
Strength 1			
Strength 2			
Strength 3			
Strength 4			
Strength 5			

Strengths Coaching Process and Tools

Each of your strengths has unique power on its own. When you combine your five strengths together you bring qualities and power that are uniquely yours. Let me give you an example.

*For me, Baha, my top five Strengths Themes are **Maximizer, Achiever, Belief, Analytical, and Communication.** When asked to describe my strengths in combination, this is what I would say:*

> "I am **a maximizer**; I love to build on the great ideas of other people and make them better. The **analytical** part of me loves to put ideas and activities into a process that is easy to follow. As an **achiever** I tend to be project oriented. I believe "**belief**" is the theology and science of strengths. In our workshops and coaching, I use my **communication** to help others know and invest their God given strengths. I believe this is my calling. I love it."

*For more on **"I was made for this"** see Exercise 20 in the Strengths Workshop book.*

How would you describe your strengths in combination? Write it in the space bellow:

> - **My top five Strengths themes are:**
> - **When asked to describe my strengths in combination this is what I would say:**

They say **"a picture is worth a thousand words."** Draw an image that reflects your strengths as you see it now or as you see it reflected in your future life. See http://strengthsschool.com/strengthsfinder-cards.

"**Tell me about yourself**" could be the most used job interview question. Suppose you have a planned meeting with a **new** leader in your church or workplace and you were asked "tell me about yourself". What would you say? This is your chance to give testimony to:

- The uniqueness of God's creation revealed in your talents and their combination

- The knowledge, skills and experiences you have gained

- The temptations and risks you experience as result of the shadow side of your strengths

Write this as a life story that you can share in 5 – 10 minutes.

15.　*What did you learn and what will you do?*

Prayerfully, ask **God** to help you define the best you have learned through the **"Communicate your Strengths"** steps? What changes would you like to do as a result? **How does this relate to your coaching objectives?**

The Best I Learned	Desired Change or Actions

- **For your Coach,** include this summary in your progress dashboard and send it to your coach before your next coaching session.

Spiritual Gifts have strong Biblical foundations. They are interpreted in many ways. There are many tools to help you discover your spiritual gifts. If you do not know your spiritual gifts take the survey at http://www.spiritualgiftstest.com/.

The same God who gave you your strengths gave you your spiritual gifts. Read the explanations and Bible references to our spiritual gifts. **Prayerfully** seek insights on how your understanding of your strengths affirms your spiritual gifts and vice versa. Use the table below to record your insights.

Spiritual Gifts	Affirming Strengths Insights

D. *Living Your Strengths*

Living your strengths is investing your strengths. According to Matthew 25, parable of the talents, you have a God given responsibility to invest your strengths where it brings the highest return and the most lasting impact. Investing your strengths is an intentional process. In the process of investing your strengths you need a vision and clear objectives of the change you want to see happen to your roles and relationships.

> Pray: "Lord, help me see how I can live in the strengths you gave me."

Note: Change requires supportive relationships. In the following section we encourage you to focus on where you are likely to have supportive roles and relationships.

16. *What do you see about your Strengths?*

Go back to your StrengthsFinder2.0 reports. There you will find ideas and examples that relate to each of your five strengths themes. See https://www.GallupStrengthCenter.com/SignIn/en-US/Index

- **Read the ideas section** for each of your strengths. Highlight ideas that you like. Write your observations in the table below.

- **Read the examples section** for each of your strengths. Highlight examples that you like. Write your observations below.

Strengths	Ideas I like	Examples I like

Strengths Coaching Process and Tools

17.   *What is your vision or dream?*

The bible says that "without a vision people perish." Everything that will ever happen will start with a vision or a dream. Watch this video https://www.youtube.com/watch?v=4vl6wCiUZYc. You may not be an artist, I am sure you can scribble, sketch and paint stick figures. Whatever creative talents you have, use them as best as you can. Follow the instructions given on this video to create an image of the change you want to see. Ask your Heavenly Father to help you.

18.   Who are your important people?

Important people share or at least appreciate your vision. They are likely to collaborate with you or at least support you in moving forward to fulfill your vision. List important people and why they could support your dream. Share your vision and record their response.

Important people	Why are they likely to support your vision?	Their response

Strengths Coaching Process and Tools

19.   Who are your teachable people?

Teachable people benefit and receive value from your vision or dream.
They are likely to have needs that can be met through your vision or
dream. They also learn or grow as you invest your strengths in them.
List teachable people and why they could benefit from your dream.
Share your vision with them and then record their response

Teachable people	Why they benefit from your vision	Their response

20.   Who are your draining people?

Draining people are those who are not among your important or teachable people. Often they are not bad people, but those who leave you drained, exhausted or helpless because they have needs that cannot be met by your top strengths. While you may not be able to totally avoid the draining people you must be intentional in containing their negative impact.

List your draining people and how you may be able to limit your exposure to their negative impact.

Teachable people	How you may limit their impact

Strengths Coaching Process and Tools

21. *Where do you spend your time?*

We measure what we value. You value your time. Do you spend enough time with your important and teachable people? Consider what changes you wish to make in the areas where you spend your time. Consider the percentage of your time spent in each of the following areas and the changes you would like to make.

	Desired change
Time for yourself	
%	
Time with Important people	
%	
Time with Teachable people	
%	
Time with draining people	
%	
Other	
%	

Prayerfully, ask **God** to help you define the best you have learned through the **"Invest Your Strengths"** steps? What changes would you like to do as a result? **How does this relate to your coaching objectives?**

The Best I Learned	Desired Change or Actions

- **For your Coach,** include this summary in your progress dashboard and send it to your coach before your next coaching session.

E. ROLES FOR YOUR STRENGTHS

Refer to the section on roles in the Strengths Workshop book.

Ill-defined roles are a key cause for stress, ineffectiveness and overloaded lives. Clearly defined roles not only improve personal and team effectiveness but also contribute greatly to healthy relationships and personal well-being.

> Pray: "Lord, help me define the roles you want me to play."

23. What role will you play?

The attached diagram illustrates the following six questions or steps that will help you write clear role descriptions. To enhance effectiveness use this process to define work, personal, family, and ministry roles. Use it to communicate your roles and the roles of your important people.

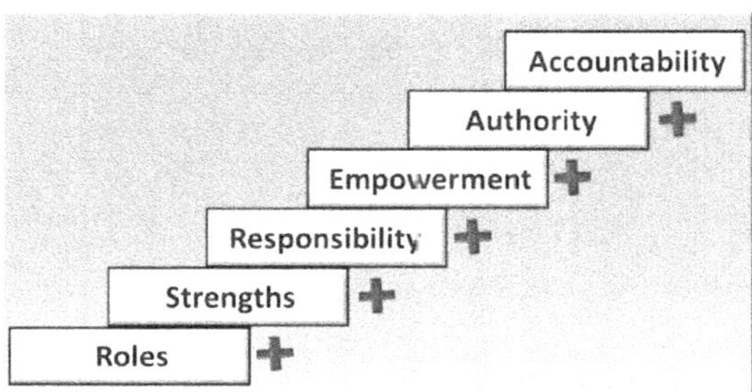

With some creativity, in all your interactions and responsib lities, use this process to define your roles. Wither you are invited to a meeting, or join a project team or even attend a community event, a ways ask, "What role am I expected to play?"

The roles you seek to play should use your existing strengths to maximum benefit and also develop your God given strengths.

A. What do you call this role?

<table>
<tr><td>

B. Which of your top strengths will you use in this role? What new competencies do you need to gain to help you in this role?

</td></tr>
<tr><td>

</td></tr>
<tr><td>

C. What is your primary responsibility and related goals?

</td></tr>
<tr><td>

</td></tr>
</table>

D. How are you empowered to play this role? Include
resources and time (see Exercise 27)

<table>
<tr><td>E.</td><td>Who gives you the authority to play this role?</td></tr>
<tr><td colspan="2">

</td></tr>
<tr><td>F.</td><td>How will you be accountable in playing this role?</td></tr>
<tr><td colspan="2">

</td></tr>
</table>

Note: Relate your thoughts to step "F: Project Plan"

24.   What factors will impact your roles?

There are positive factors that will enhance your ability to play your roles. There will also be negative factors that may hinder your ability to play your roles. In the table below, list:

- the positive factors and how you may leverage them to advantage
- the negative factors and how you may mitigate against them

Positive Factors	How I will leverage them

Negative Factors	How I will mitigate against them

In relationship to this specific role, discovering the strengths of your important people will do wonders to how you appreciate, communicate and collaborate with each other. Use the same process and tools you used to discover you lowest and lesser strengths. **(See step 3 and 4)** The difference is that as you read the description of each of the 34 Strengths themes, you need to identify which theme best describes **one** important person. Once you identify the strengths of your important person, read the description noting adjectives or statements that best describe him. Also try to identify possible strengths. Use the following list to write your discovery.

Name	Adjectives or terms that describe my important person	Possible Strengths

Note: Share your discovery with your important person. This can be most affirming. **Do not be disappointed if he/she disagrees with your discovery.** Encourage them to take StrengthsFinder2.0.

    Strengths Coaching Process and Tools

The following table is based on the Gallup Four Domains of Strengths.

Executing	Influencing	Relationship	Strategic Thinking
· Achiever	· Activator	· Adaptability	· Analytical
· Arranger	· Command	· Developer	· Context
· Belief	· Communication	· Connectedness	· Futuristic
· Consistency	· Competition	· Empathy	· Ideation
· Deliberative	· Maximizer	· Harmony	· Input
· Discipline	· Self-Assurance	· Includer	· Intellection
· Focus	· Significance	· Individualization	· Learner
· Responsibility	· Woo	· Positivity	· Strategic
· Restorative		· Relator	

Refer to description in the Strengths Workshop book Appendix.

Consider your one important person:

- On the above grid, compare your strengths to those of your important person placing appropriate initials beside strengths.

- Consider one area where you share a common purpose or vision.

- Discuss how your strengths **can play complimentary roles and summarize your observations below.**

Prayerfully, ask **God** to help you define the best you have learned through the "**Roles for your Strengths**" steps? What changes would you like to do as a result? **How does this relate to your coaching objectives?**

The Best I Learned	Desired Change or Actions

- **For your Coach,** include this summary in your progress dashboard and send it to your coach before your next coaching session.

F. LIFE PLANS

Change never happens without a plan. Our book, *Life Plans,* offers more than 20 different plans that you can use to bring about change to various aspects of your life. At our eStore you may get a gift copy of this book. **See** http://estore.strengthsworkshop.ca/product/lp-ebook.

There are two approaches to bring about healthy life changes:

- Change in operational routine or behavioral habits such as going to bed earlier, eating less junk food, taking a walk each day…

- Project oriented changes that have predefined objectives and goals such as saving for a new car, losing 15 pounds …

Exercising what you have learned so far is best applied to new or existing projects. Projects have well defined purpose, objectives and structures. They are time dependent having a beginning and an end. They offer you an opportunity to collaborate with others who compliment your strengths.

Projects by nature have constraints and require a plan. The attached **Jigsaw Puzzle diagrams** highlight the interdependence of each of these constraints. Using the following questions create project plan where you can communicate, apply, and grow your strengths.

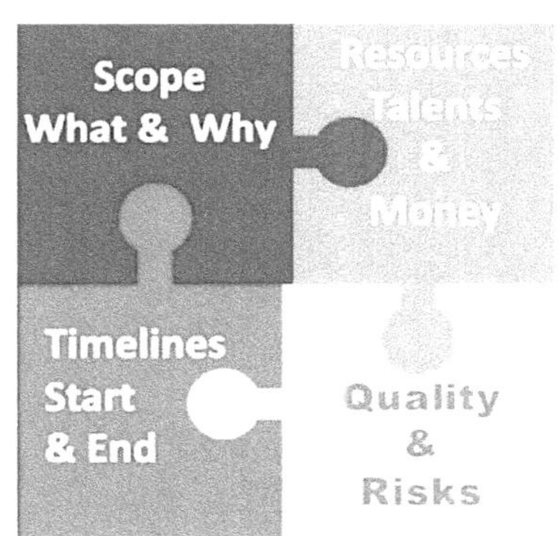

Consider a **simple, short term** project that responds to your passions and impacts your **roles and supportive relationships**. This will give you the ability to find opportunities where you can develop your strengths and enhance your relationships. Later you can apply what you have learned to more complicated projects, roles, and relationships.

28. *What is the project scope?*

The following project scope questions help you understand, communicate, and agree on the purpose, value, and project results.

> **A.** **What do you call this project?**

B. What is the project vison and purpose?

C. Who are the people that will be impacted by this project?

D. What are the expected goals or results of this project?

29. What resources do you need?

Resources are the empowering part of your role on this project. Every project needs a diverse mix of financial and material resources as well as human capital. Human capital is reflected in the right **team strength (Talents X knowledge, skills and experience)** and the expected time investment. Use the following questions to help you paint a picture of the required resources:

A. What finances, materials, and tools are needed for this project?

B. What roles and how much time is needed for each role?

D. What strengths are required for these roles?

E. What role will you play? Relate to your strengths. Exercise 21

There are risks associated with any change and every project. Having the right level of detail reduces project risks. But excessive quality controls and administrative details result in burdensome costs.

While some projects by their nature require 100% accuracy and quality controls, the **Pareto principle,** suggests that 80% of the quality benefits can be achieved through 20% of the most critical project elements. 80% of the risks can be avoided by 20% of the needed controls. To reduce costs always seek simplicity.

What are the qualities and risk factors that you need to consider?

31. What are the project timelines?

Project timelines take you closer into the steps and tasks required to deliver the needed project results and benefits. Here we examine the **elapsed time** or the time between starting the project and when it ends. Here we must also examine the time needed for the various **work breakdown structures** and related tasks. Work breakdown structures answer a key question, "What are the major parts of the project, how do they relate to each other, or how are they dependent on each other". The table below is sometimes called a Gantt chart.

WBS T#	MILESTONE Task or Action	Key Roles/ Resources	Start Date	End Date
A- 1				
2				
3				
4				
5				
5				
B-6				
7				
8				
9				
10				
C-11				
12				
13				
14				
15				

Strengths Coaching Process and Tools

32. *What did you learn and what will you do?*

Prayerfully, ask **God** to help you define the best you have learned through the "**Action plan**" steps? What changes would you like to do as a result? **How does this relate to your coaching objectives?**

The Best I Learned	Desired Change or Actions

- **For your Coach,** include this summary in your progress dashboard and send it to your coach before your next coaching session.

Go to http://estore.strengthsworkshop.ca/welcome/gd. You will find webinars offered by leading coaches and scientists for each strength. Record any additional insights you gain on your understanding and application of your strengths.

Strengths	Insights

At http://integrity-plus.com/SM/Notes/TST.xlsx you can download an MS Excel program that gives you a pie diagram of your strengths based on the **Four Strengths Domains priority of your top 5 strengths**. FIRST READ the instruction page. Enter your data and examine the pie image.

- What does this pie image tell you?

- How is this reflected in your present roles?

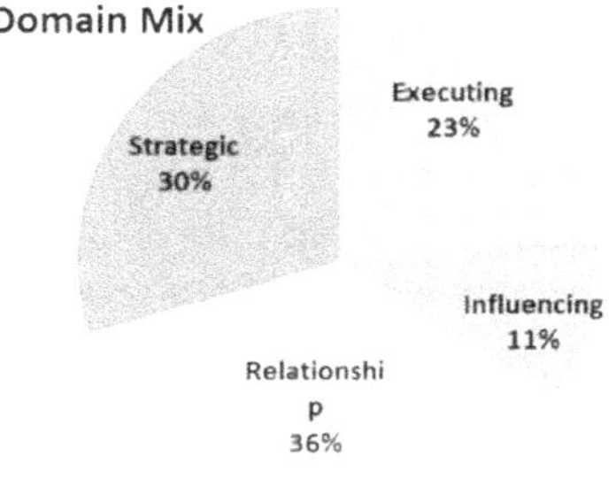

This simple tool can be a very effective communication tool. You may use it to illustrate the strengths of your important people. Go further and enter the strengths of your team members in a group page.

- What does this tell you about the strengths of your group?

- How does the strengths of your group relate to the purpose and objectives of your team?

- Do you see opportunities for change or enhancements?

This is your opportunity to be a champion for strengths in your organization. Take a lead. Coach someone. The impact you can have is greater than you will ever imagine.

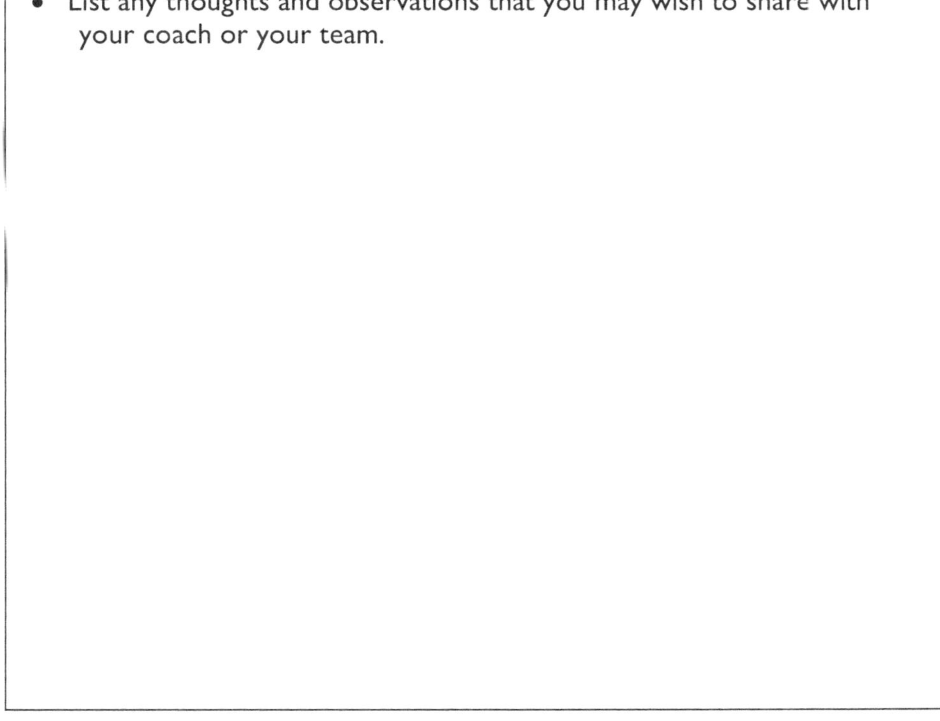

- List any thoughts and observations that you may wish to share with your coach or your team.

In a few simple words, coaching is one person helping another discover how he can achieve desired change. In Biblical terms coaching is one of the ways we apply Christ's command in Matthew 28, "**Go and make disciples.**" Paid or unpaid we are all called to go and make disciples. We are all called to coach.

In his book "The Lost Art of Mentoring" renowned leader Ted Enstrom says *"Everyone needs a Paul and everyone must have Timothy."* Dr. Al Winsman of Gallup puts it in different words by saying, *"Everyone needs a coach and every one can coach."* At its heart this statement is totally true, but to excel in developing a coaching practice hinges on identifying your **coaching fit or sweet spot**. In Christ Centered Coaching we partner with the spirit of Christ to identify this fit or sweet spot.

If you sense the call of Jesus to invest in one-on-one focused, disciplined discipleship relationships you should consider coaching. **Paid or unpaid,** coaching is an opportunity for you to be a good steward of your God given strengths. In Strengths coaching you use your God given strengths to help someone else discover his or her strengths and apply them to achieve desired healthy change in roles and/or relationships.

Yes, everyone can coach. With some practice you can find your right fit. You can excel as a Strengths coach if:

- you are intentional in growing and developing your own strengths
- you are interested in using your understanding of your own talents to help others on their life journey
- you are clear in understanding the kind of client needs that you may be able to serve
- you are likely to be organized and committed to investing the time to interact with people about their strengths
- you are able to see the good in others
- you are genuinely interested and comfortable interacting with people you do not know well
- you are good listener, not only to spoken words but also more importantly to tone and body language
- you are willing to build warm relationships and put people at ease
- you are curious by asking questions that help people discover answers to their own challenges

If you see yourself in many of the above statements you are likely a person who:

- gains satisfaction from investing in others and seeing them grow

- finds pleasure in helping people capitalize on what they do well
- has the admiration of others and challenges them to ask you about your process of discovery
- provides a model of what is possible for others who can become your clients or disciples
- can find indicators of a possible fit with a potential client or disciples if you prayerfully seek for them.

If that is you, the following discussion questions are for you   They are designed to help you consider developing an intentional coaching practice. These follow the thoughts presented in the Christ Centered Coaching booklet and follow the same structure presented in the following diagram. See http://estore.strengthsworkshop.ca/product/coach-2.

The Coach

What are your Strengths?

Knowing your strengths is the first step in developing your coaching practice. Start by practicing what you preach. Follow the six step Strengths process. Once completed, summarize the "**Tell me about yourself**" exercise.

In few short sentences that reflect how this process has helped you know your strengths and how it is leading you to a coaching practice. In other words, if approached by someone who could be your coaching client what would you say in response to "tell me about yourself"?

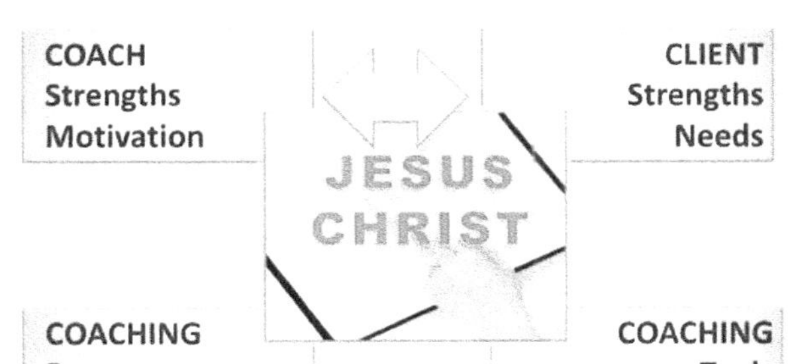

The fact that you know your strengths will help you:

- understand the kind of client needs that you may be able to serve
- gain the admiration of others and challenge them to ask you about your process of discovery
- provide a model of what is possible for others who can become your clients
- see indicators of a possible fit with a possible client

With your coaching practice in mind, in the space below start writing your answer to **"Tell me about yourself."**

Strengths Coaching Process and Tools

How are you different from other coaches?

In response to growing demand, the coaching industry has mushroomed. There is a variety of coaching organizations to train you and sell you coaching tools. The value of such relationships should be examined in light of your vision, but more importantly the kind of clients you seek to serve.

Similar to other professions, **success hinges on having the right fit** and ability to differentiate yourself in the mind of a specific group of clients. This is an evolving process.

With your coaching practice in mind think of the clients you want to coach, what makes you different in their sight? Could it be: your talents, your values, your knowledge, your skills, your experience, or even your lower fees… In the space bellow start writing few points.

What are your motivations?

Everything starts with a dream or a need that motivates you. In other words why do you want to coach? How you see your coaching practice 2–3 years from today. Highlight the basic drivers for your vision. Picture yourself sharing this with your important and teachable people.

Like any other profession, a coaching practice has initial investments and ongoing costs. It is critical that you articulate the expected rewards and possible costs including **material, financial, time ...**

Dreams and Motivators	Costs

Strengths Coaching Process and Tools

What are your objectives?

Objectives add structure to your dreams and present solutions responding to your needs. Objectives are statements of faith of what you would like to see happen at a future point. Consider the next 12 months. In the space below list three key objectives and why they are important to you. If your motivation is financial, list the minimum and maximum desired income in light of your projected costs.

Prioritized Coaching Objectives	Why they are important

What roles do you wish to play?

Being clear on the coaching roles you wish to play is a critical success factor. As a coach you may play the role of an advisor, listener, sounding board, catalyst, visionary, problem solver, accountability point… Having clear roles is critical to finding the best fit to the clients you wishes to coach. Below prioritize and describe 3–4 roles you would like to play.

Role	Description (75 words or less)

Strengths Coaching Process and Tools

How do you describe your ideal client?

Strengths Coaches help clients understand, own, and apply their strengths to bring about the desired life change. The following diagram illustrates that change is a result of a thinking and ownership process.

While the client may be interested in the **idea** for change, he must acquire the **desire** to change before you can have any coaching relationship. Change always has a price. The client must be **willing** to pay the price

for change before he can move forward with a coaching relationship. As a coach you will ind that sometimes cultural, financial or other factors may hinder or elude the client's **ability** to change.

As a coach you need to help your client negotiate the obstacles he or she may encounter in moving through the above steps. Sometimes the client may be challenged in acquiring the desire or willingness to change because he or she has not identified clear needs. In such a case the **"how are you"** tool is a good first step to discerning needs. At other points you may find the exercise of developing a vision or a dream to be a good, helpful first step. Other options may include a conversation around core values or roles and their related exercises. **All of these conversations can be introductory to engaging in a Strengths coaching relationship.**

Fit is critical. Once the coaching need and objectives are defined, your role is holding the responsibility of moving forward or disengaging from the coaching relationship. It is highly advisable and professional to clearly communicate your fit to your client needs. Discerning this fit may start by comparing the client need to your areas of knowledge, skills and or experience. Coaching style, proximity and availability are also factors that may help define your client fit.

> In the space below list key points that describe the clients that could fit in your coaching sweet spot.

The Tools

Coaching is referred to as a professional practice. In this practice we are all learning, developing, and growing. The tools provided in this supplement provide you with a good starting point. As you grow in your practice, you will modify them and blend them to your own style and the specific needs of your sweet spot clients. The reality is that just as you are unique, each client is unique. The result is that there will never be a perfect tool.

While we encourage you to modify these tools and acquire new tools, we advise you against the risk of the overloaded toolbox. Learning the effective use of tools requires time. Having too many tools has a high cost in time and may add complexity and administrative overhead that you can not afford.

The Process

There are two processes that we may reference here. The first process involves finding the right clients. This is often called **"business development process"** or **"client development process."** The second is the delivery of services or the coaching process.

What is your client development process?

Finding the right clients is often one of the challenges faced by many coaches. Coaches are often reluctant or unable to promote their practice. There are several steps that you need to consider in building your coaching practice:

1. **Exposure:** It is critical that you start by letting people know of your interest, knowledge and competence in a specific subject or issue that has a broad appeal or responds a pervasive real need. For exposure you may consider:
   - Writing and speaking about overloaded lives, strengths, roles …
   - Networking and social media platforms
   - Referrals by pastors or other professionals
   - Having "a hook" by asking good leading questions for example:
     - Tell me about yourself?
     - Why is it that most people do not love their work?
     - How do you describe your strengths?
     - What do you love to do?
     - What changes would you like to see in your roles or relationships?

    Strengths Coaching Process and Tools

<table>
<tr><td>What exposure tools or strategies can you use?</td></tr>
<tr><td>

</td></tr>
</table>

2. **Connection:** To make a connection to possible clients you need to offer a low risk opportunity to become exposed to how you may be of help. This can take the form of:

- A free white paper on a related subject
- A free assessment survey
- A low cost seminar such as the strengths workshop video seminar.
- A low cost group coaching engagement such as the Strengths Workshop six week small group experience
- A free introductory coaching session

<table>
<tr><td>What connection tools or strategies can you use?</td></tr>
<tr><td>

</td></tr>
</table>

Note: Do not let the free stuff devalue your services.

3. **Selection:** The selection process is where you and the client work together to ensure that there is a fit for a credible coaching relationship. This is often done through the initiation phase. The discovery exercises are good starting tools. In Strengths Coaching the initiation includes:

   - Taking the StrengthsFinder2.0 assessment
   - Providing the client with a copy of this supplement
   - Helping the client define the amount of time he or she is willing to commit to this plan
   - Completing the coaching agreement

What selection tools or strategies can you use?

   Strengths Coaching Process and Tools

Strengths Workshop for client development

Over the past years we have offered the Strengths Workshop in half day and full day sessions to groups of differing sizes in different cultures, mission and ministry teams. At the end of each workshop session we always ask for evaluation and feedback comments. In addition, we also ask the participants to indicate if they would be interested in follow-up activities in the form of **one-on-one coaching or being part of an application oriented small group.** We are pleased to report that on average about 50% of the participants indicate interest in some form of follow-up. Based on this experience we suggest that the Strengths Workshop offers an excellent client engagement process. As illustrated in the attached diagram, this process allows you to engage with clients based on their own needs and time availability.

Strengths Development Options

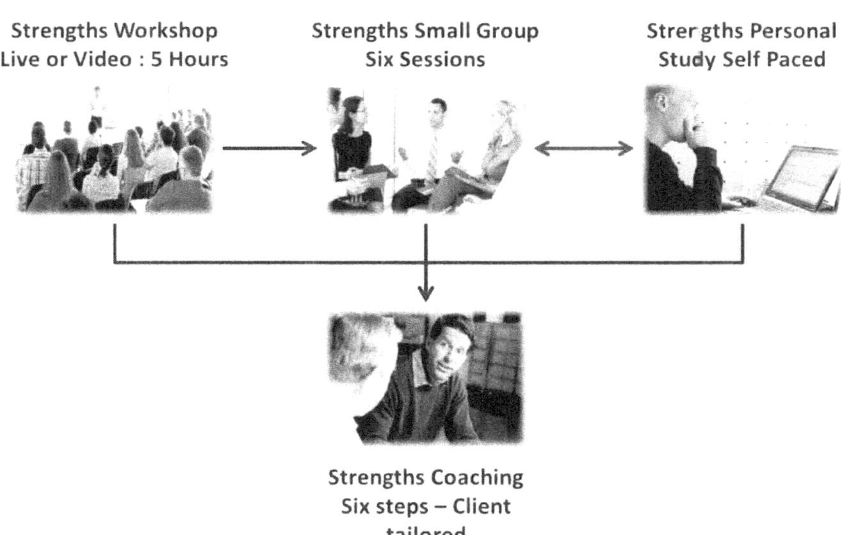

- **The Strengths Workshop:** Live or video about 5 hours
  http://integrity-plus.com/wp/sm/sw/
- **The Strengths Small Group:** Six 90 minute sessions
  http://integrity-plus.com/wp/sm/sg/
- **Strengths Personal study:** Client paced http://integrity-plus.com/wp/sm/sp/
- **Strengths coaching:** format can be a good connection service and tool. http://integrity-plus.com/wp/sm/coaching/

Client Development Project

Client development is a project. Use the structure outlined in step six to develop your own. This is your chance to exercise your talents one more time.

The Coaching Process

The attached diagram illustrates a generic coaching process which we describe in the Christ Centered Coaching booklet. This diagram also illustrates the **I G R O W** process with is used to direct each coaching conversation and the related progress dashboard template referenced in other parts of this document.

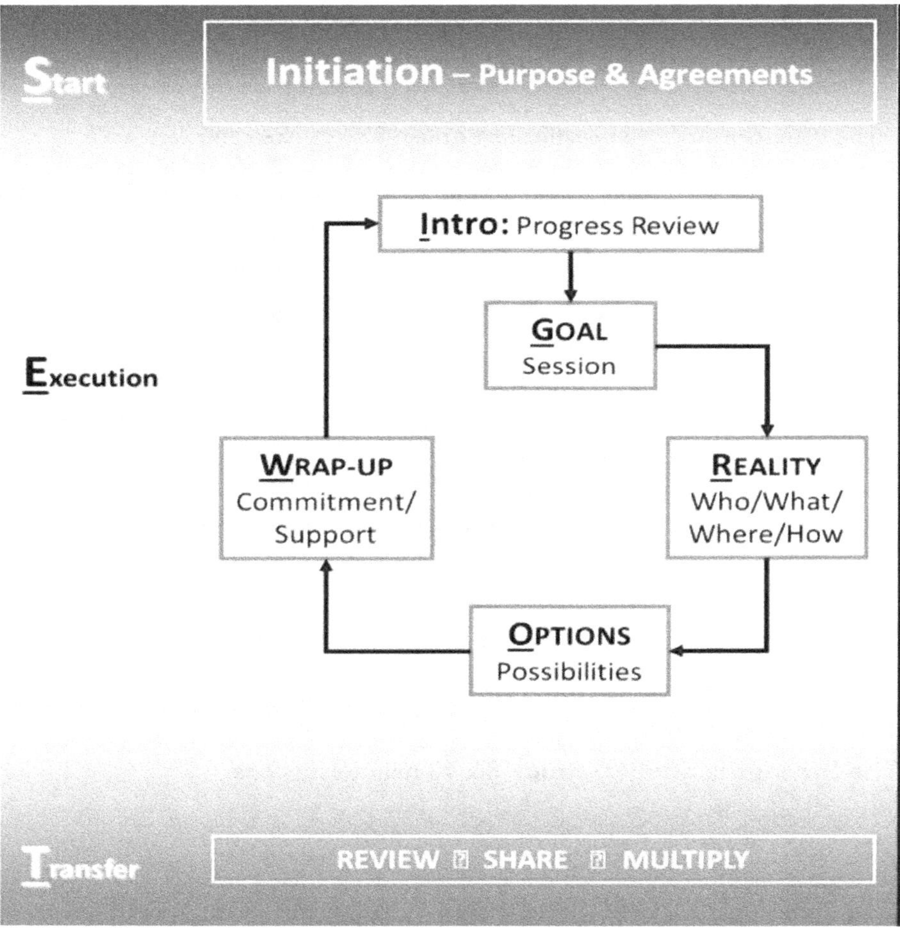

    Strengths Coaching Process and Tools

Do you need a coaching agreement?

Written or not, you must have a coaching agreement. This does not need to be complicated. The following is an example of a simple coaching agreement

The purpose of our coaching relationship is to help you know and communicate your strengths with authenticity and invest your strengths in roles where they can grow and be most effective.

A. **Term, Progress:**
   1. **Term:** As much as possible this coaching relationship will be set for 12 to 24 weeks.
   2. **Progress:** Progress will be monitored using a modified **Progress Dashboard and the session effectiveness scores.** If either party believes that coaching is ineffective, this agreement may be terminated.
   3. **Confidentiality:** To protect confidentiality and trust the client is responsible to communicate the terms and progress of this coaching relationship as necessary.
   4. **No legal or personal liability is provided or assumed on the part of the coach.**
   5. **When, where, and how:**

Frequency How Often:		When Day/ Time		Format BY Phone/In Person	

B. **Fees:**

- As our client, to gain expected benefits it is important that you are invested in this coaching process.
- **Our fees to you** will be based on your ability or desire to donate to our **Latin America Ministry projects. They are tax deductible donations.**
- Our normal fees to our business clients are listed on our web site. See http://www.integrity-plus.com/wp/resources/fees/
- Agreed rate $__________ per hour

Agreed by Coach: Baha Habashy on   *Agreed by Client: Add Client Name on*

Date: *Date:*

As a summary, this is a supplement to Christ Centered Coaching available at http://estore.strengthsworkshop.ca/product/coach-2. Remember:

- You must be true to living and growing your own strengths. Honesty and authenticity is the bedrock of any personal coaching relationship.
- The Strengths Coaching Process provides a model for a focused coaching relationship.
- Your client must define the coaching objectives. Your role is to control the process towards achieving the objectives.
- The I **G R O W** model and the progress dashboard will direct each coaching conversation. To insure that each coaching conversation moves you closer to achieving the coaching objectives, your client provides the goal of each coaching session. This should relate to the coaching objectives.
- Developing your coaching skill hinges on **effective listening** and **asking good questions**. As you invest in developing these skills they will serve you well in all aspects of your life.
- Become a student of strengths by going deeper in understanding your client's strengths.
- The videos at http://estore.strengthsworkshop.ca/welcome/gd are a great tool to enhance your understanding of each Strength theme.
- Become familiar with each of the exercises provided in the process. Go through them for yourself.
- Your objective is to help your client develop and execute a realistic Strengths Coaching plan using the six steps provided in the supplement. **See the introduction.**
- You must help your client see that he should commit to spend **2–4 hours per week**. This should:
  - Allow him or her to do as many exercises as possible every week.
  - Meet with you **weekly or bi weekly** 30–90 minutes.
- You and your client must prioritize the important roles you can play in this process. For example you may play the role of **encourager, accountability source, Catalyst, Sounding board …**
- As you grow your practice, your effective coaching toolbox evolves to respond to your client needs as well as your coaching sweet spot. The coaching questions in this supplement are your starting points.
- Always encourage your client to share what he or she is learning with others. This will do wonders for his or her development.

- Around mid-point, encourage your client to consider coaching someone else.
- To help you in your coaching process at http://integrity-plus.com/Data/Templates/CoachingProfile.docx you may download a sample client profile document. This document will help you capture the most critical client profile elements. Use the progress dashboard to record notes from each coaching conversation.

Other Resources

For Coaches who wish to learn more, there are many outstanding authors on the subject of coaching. Their books offer helpful methodologies, tools, and templates. Here are a few we recently used:

- Jane Creswell, *Christ-Centered Coaching*. St. Louis, MI: Chalice Press, 2006.
- Downey, Myles. *Effective Coaching: Lessons from the Coach's Coach.* South Melbourne, Australia: Cengage Learning, 2003.
- Stoltzfus, Tony. *Coaching Questions: A Coach's Guide to Powerful Asking Skills.* Virginia Beach, VA: Tony Stoltzfus, 2008.
- Stoltzfus, Tony. *Leadership Coaching: The Disciplines, Skills and Heart of a Christian Coach.* Virginia Beach, VA: Tony Stoltzfus, 2005.
- Ted W. Engstrom, *The Lost Art Of Mentoring.* Newburgh, IN: Trinity Press, 2000.
- Whitmore, John. *Coaching for Performance: Growing People, Performance and Purpose.* London: Nicholas Brealey Publishing, 2004.
- Whitworth, Laura. *Co-Active Coaching: New Skills for Coaching People Toward Success in Work and Life.* Mountain View, California: Davies-Black Publishing, *1998.*
- Professional life Coaching; American Association of Christian Counselors and Light University.

http://www.aacc.net/courses/life-coaching/life_coaching_enroll/

Our Books – Our Gifts

Our books have been written to play a role in our coaching practice. Most of their content is based on the workshops that we were engaged to deliver to business and ministry teams since 2001. Our books are a collection of thoughts, tips, and tools. These tools come in the form of thinking and communication exercises and templates.

Print copies are available at Amazon.com or our eStore. As part of our free Strengths Ministry, we are glad to offer our books in Pdf format as additional free tools for you to use. See http://estore.strengthsworkshop.ca/?page_id=404

<table>
<tr>
<td></td>
<td>

THE STRENGTHS WORKSHOP

Grow Your Strengths and Live Your Callings

Biblically based and building on the Gallup StrengthsFinder assessment this book is designed to help you discover your God given Strengths so you can fulfil your life callings.

ISBN 978-0-9736493-2-1

</td>
</tr>
<tr>
<td>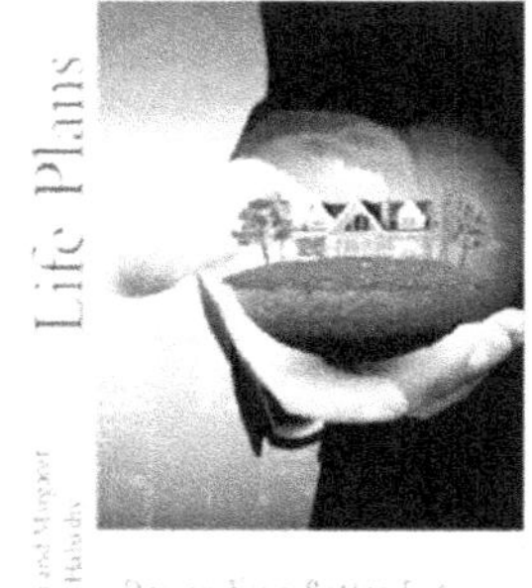</td>
<td>

LIFE PLANS

Design Your Better Future

Using the model of house building this book contains a collection of 22 plans relating to most aspects of personal and work life.

ISBN : 978-0-9736493-5-2

</td>
</tr>
<tr>
<td>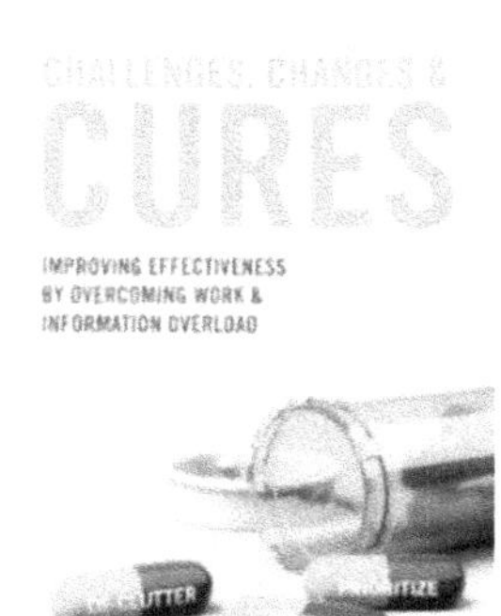</td>
<td>

CHALLENGES, CHANGES & CURES

Improving Effectiveness by Overcoming Work and Information Overload

Dealing with work habits this book is designed help you communicate, delegate, and collaborate more effectively in the workplace.

Paperback ISBN 978-0-9736493-4-5

</td>
</tr>
</table>

END NOTES

[1] True story modified for illustration

[2] Myles Downey, *Effective Coaching: Lessons from the Coaches 'Coach* (South Melbourne, Australia: Cengage Learning, 2003), 59.

[3] Tony Stoltzfus, *Coaching Questions: A Coach's Guide to Powerful Asking Skills* (Virginia Beach, VA: Tony Stoltzfus, 2008), 7.

[4] Gary D. Chapman, *The Five Love Languages: How to Express Heartfelt Commitment to Your Mate* (Chicago: Northfield Publishing 1995).

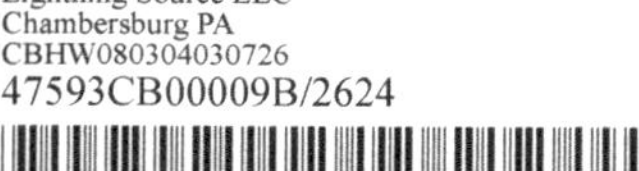